The Story of Emily the Cow

Bovine Bodhisattva

authorHOUSE®

AuthorHouse™
1663 Liberty Drive, Suite 200
Bloomington, IN 47403
www.authorhouse.com
Phone: 1-800-839-8640

First published by AuthorHouse 8/24/2007

ISBN: 978-1-4259-7593-7 (sc)

Library of Congress Control Number: 2006909681

Printed in the United States of America
Bloomington, Indiana

This book is printed on acid-free paper.

Bovine Bodhisattva

Bo·vine (bō'vīn', -vēn')

adj.
Of, relating to, or resembling a ruminant mammal of
the genus *Bos,* such as an ox, cow, or buffalo.

n.
An animal of the genus *Bos.*
[Late Latin bovīnus, from Latin bōs, bov-, cow.]

Bo·dhi·satt·va (bō'dĭ-sŭt'və)

n. Buddhism.
An enlightened being who, out of compassion,
forgoes nirvana in order to save others.

[Sanskrit bodhisattvaḥ, one whose essence is enlightenment : bodhiḥ,
perfect *knowledge* + *sattvam, essence, being (from sat-, existing).]*

*The title Bovine Bodhisattva was suggested by photographer Joan
Hill who assisted in organizing the photos for this book.*

ACKNOWLEGEMENTS

A heartfelt thank you to the dozens of people of gave so generously of their time, talents, energy, finances, and most importantly their love, that this book be assembled, published and distributed.

To those who cared for and loved Emily, and the countless people who, having developed a relationship with her, sought to end the practice of eating animals, we congratulate you. You now know what it means to practice true compassion and you understand the true meaning of peaceful coexistence.

And a special thanks to the anonymous donor (whose first name is Emily) who offered to pay off the balance on the mortgage of the Sacred Cow Animal Rights Memorial. May it continue in perpetuity to tell the story of Emily the Cow in an effort to spread vegetarianism throughout the world.

We also would like to express our sincere appreciation to the following publications (photographers acknowledged under their photos) for the rights to reprint articles about Emily's legendary journey from the slaughterhouse to the hearts of millions of people:

Associated Press
Animals' Agenda (Institute for Animals and Society)
AWI (Animal Welfare Institute)
Best Friends Magazine
The Boston Globe
The Boston Herald
Boston Vegetarian Society Newsletter
CNC Newpapers / Middlesex News / MetroWest Daily News
Culture and Animal Foundation
InCity Times
India Abroad
Parade Magazine
Peacework Magazine (American Friends Service Committee)
People Magazine

*All Proceeds from the sale of this book are used
for the care and maintenance of the*

Sacred Cow Animal Rights Memorial

on the grounds of The Peace Abbey in Sherborn, Massachusetts

TABLE OF CONTENTS

EMILY STRUGGLES TO SURVIVE CANCER

APPENDIX

This book is dedicated to the spirit of compassion that prompts people to give up eating animals and to choose a plant-based diet that promotes personal health and the sustainable health of the planet.

Herein is the life story of Emily the cow.

Open to any chapter, as each article was written to stand alone.

These articles appeared independently in newspaper and magazine accounts published both nationally and internationally about a remarkable individual who touched the lives of all who met her.

The introduction offers the reader an overview of the basic events to which the newspaper and magazine articles refer.

The order of the articles is chronological; the first 8 chapters detail Emily's escape and 40 days eluding capture. Chapter 9 through 61 cover her life in sanctuary at the Peace Abbey over a period of 8 years. Chapters 62 to 82 record her struggle with cancer, her passing, her burial and memorial service, and the placing of Emily's statue over her grave.

The book concludes with important scholarly theological considerations that may provide food for thought to the reader.

INTRODUCTION
Emily the Emissary of Compassion
SHE WAS A COW BEFORE HER TIME

By Steven Baer

It must have taken all she had – she must have been clearly aware of the fact that "it was now or never." Emily bolted from the killing floor, and with her 1,600-pound physique focused upon survival, the former dairy cow jumped a 5-foot high gate out of the slaughterhouse and escaped to spend over a month in the snowy woods. The jump and escape were tantamount to you as a dark haired political prisoner passing armed guards and security fences, and then negotiating your way through a country of light haired people with whom you have a language barrier. Emily eluded police, slaughterhouse workers and animal control officers for 40 days and 40 nights.

Emily was a two year old cow that could not produce milk. The milk industry's decision was business as usual. Unuseful and unprofitable dairy cows are rounded up and disposed of. Dairy cows are usually slaughtered when they are 5 or 6 years old because their milk production declines. Cows can, on average, live to be 25 years old. The practice is equivalent to killing a man at 20 years of age because he begins to slow down on a factory assembly line. Cows are walked, hydraulically winched, or hoisted by backhoe onto trucks, or into trailers. They are brought to places and sold intact, or brought to slaughterhouses to be sold in pieces. On their way to slaughter, cows often stand in their own excrement; they are often exposed to extreme weather in open trucks; and they are often traumatized by the demands placed upon them.

Cows that are too sick or weak to walk, even when beaten or shocked with electric prods, are called "downers." This condition may result from the trauma of a cow being pushed beyond her physical limit. A "downer" may also be indicative of a more serious disease, such as "Mad Cow

Disease," which has Alzheimer-type symptoms in humans. Pressured to keep animal parts production lines moving quickly, slaughterhouse workers respond with impatience to cows that are struggling in fright. As a result, slaughterhouses have been known to dismember and skin cows alive. "Cattle," I was told by an ex-cattle rancher named Howard Lyman, "could tell when they got close to the slaughterhouse. They know before the trailer stops... they get fidgety as they recognize the sounds and smells of their own in the slaughterhouse." "Perhaps they are reacting to the death of their own," I commented, "and felt anxious of what lay in store for them." I've seen videos recorded at slaughterhouses, and heard of cows being forcefully removed from transport, forced into the buildings of death, and dismembered alive, sometimes conscious, as they often hung upside down by a hoof.

It was amid the chaos of this assaultive violence that Emily decided she had seen, heard, and smelled enough to know that this was the type of treatment she did not want to experience. In a traditional "fight or flight" decision, Emily concluded that it was not in her best interest to pursue an aggressive, non-cooperative demeanor, so she optioned for flight. And fly she did. Emily was minutes away from becoming another nameless, faceless casualty in the line of violent attacks and deaths at a Massachusetts slaughterhouse when she made her leap on November 14, 1995.

By jumping the 5-foot gate at the slaughterhouse, Emily bound her way to freedom. She escaped from the sounds, perhaps the farewell pleas, of the other cows she may have known, who were calling out in fearful agony. Perhaps the connection between the smells of torn flesh, nervous sweat, and the feeling of anxiety as desperate calls from cows turned silent motivated her to search for an exit and flee.

Over a 5 foot gate leading out of the building Emily dove, and into the woods of a suburban area. What happened next is remarkable. Emily needed to learn how to survive and quickly. Winter was already upon New England. There was an early frost that November. On the farm, cows are given hay; there is little need to forage. On factory farms, cows aren't allowed to forage, it takes too much effort to move the cows, or what businessmen refer to as "the milking units" into the barn to be milked. She probably only knew a life of being portioned food by an agribusiness farmer. Being able to find her own food in the snow and cold was required now for her survival. Compounding her poor chances of survival were the people from the slaughterhouse who were looking for her, and there were town officials looking for her, and there were opportunists who wanted her for reward money or worse.... for her body parts. But there were also friends. People who would set out food for her, and people who were searching for her to protect her from our violent society... a society so ingrained with abusive and harmful thoughts about animals that they felt justified in their unflinching belief that a cow has no right to exist except as a vehicle for the next glass of milk, or the next burger at a fast food joint... billions and billions sold - on the idea that killing innocent life is acceptable, millions and millions dead because unlike Emily they weren't able to jump to freedom.

Emily managed to evade them all for five weeks. Judging from her tracks in the December snow and stories of sightings, she joined a herd of deer – an association that afforded her a level of safety in numbers from a number of predators – including human. Emily, the fugitive, became a local folk hero aided and abetted by local residents who began watching out for her and leaving offerings of hay out for her and the deer in their back yards. But with the arctic temperatures of early December already gnawing on face and hoof, who among the cow-friendly community would adopt her and provide her with shelter?

One family who was searching for Emily had long before recognized the connection between human suffering and animal suffering, between nation at war with nation, and human at war with animal, between social injustice and injustice to animals – that family was the Randas of the Peace Abbey. Meg and Lewis Randa set out to make a difference in Emily's life. They decided to bring Emily home to a sanctuary, away from suffering.

To insure Emily's safety, to insure that the slaughterhouse would not try to claim Emily if the Randas managed to encourage Emily to come out of the forest with them, the Randa's first had to show tolerance for the unjust rules of the land – the rule that says animals are considered property under the law.

Laws which are born of people who surround themselves with the notion that the emotional and physical needs of "the other" are inconsequential, or that consideration for "the other" should be quickly dismissed as childish, are subject to great correction in the light of a bit of education. Whether it is the institution of slavery in the 1700's, or the mistreatment of women in the 1800's or the abuse of animals in the 1900's, it is the unjust rules of the land, laws biased in favor of the insensitive, popularized by threat of force or convenience of personal gain, that allow for the continuity of immoral and unjust considerations to occur. Why was it just to treat a black man as property in the 1700's?

Why was it just to treat a woman as property in the 1800's? And why was it just to treat animals as property in the 1900's? Black men had to buy their freedom; women had to negotiate their freedom; and animals... animals are still not free. Perhaps the best chance an animal has to be free is to educate his or her enslavers, to bring awareness to us humans, to narrow the barrier of distance that humans have placed between themselves and the natural world, and let the humans know... Hey! I feel, I think, I bleed, I ache... I am like you... treat me like you treat yourself... treat me with compassion. The Randas understood that about animals and people.

The paying of money to redeem or save the life of a living being, whether that being is a kidnapped sister or a cow slated for slaughter, wrongfully enforces the concept that a life can be reduced to the level of a commodity, a thing that may be bought or sold or applied significance only in proportion to a monetary worth. No matter how distasteful and unconscionable the philosophy and the practice, it was required of Meg and Lewis Randa under the present system of barbaric laws in this country in order to obtain their right to pursue their desire to protect Emily.

Because the Randas were respected as people who treated others with compassion and with fairness, and because the community surrounding the slaughterhouse had bonded with Emily through the excellent and sympathetic coverage she received in the Middlesex News, Frank Arena the owner of the Arena Slaughterhouse, in an unexpected twist, agreed to sell the cow valued at $500 for just $1. He said, "those people [the Randas] wanted it for a good cause." The Arenas even offered to help find Emily for the Randas and capture her. Joanne Arena said her father was moved by all the public support for Emily.

Once the legalities were taken care of the Randas had to find Emily.

With the help of compassionate neighbors Bill and Rose Abbott and Bob Ahern, the Randas spent snowy afternoons trying to lure Emily from her hiding place. Then they had to gain Emily's trust which over the course of days they engaged Emily as an equal – as a spirit who needed loving arms and engaging words and non-violent thoughts. All these the Randas provided, and more. On Christmas Eve December

24, 1995 after being in the woods for 40 days and having dropped 500 pounds to weigh nearly 1,200 pounds, Emily accepted a ride with the Randas back to the Peace Abbey.

A celebratory non-violent meal consisting of vegan foods was shared with Emily by her new family, the Randas. Emily finally ended her flight and began domestic life with the Randas. Emily joined a horse and 2 goats, as she settled into her barn at the Sherborn Peace Abbey.

The Randa's work was just beginning. The Randas learned quickly what Emily needed to not only survive, but more so, to excel. Emily was a patient teacher.

Meg Randa was told that, "The Hindu community all think she is a messenger to the world to be compassionate."

Beyond the regular daily care and attention Emily required, and the Randas enthusiastically provided, Emily showed an interest in being an ambassador for compassion, so the Randas created opportunities for the public relations exposure she craved. Thus she began her life as New England's most famous cow. Emily had her own newspaper column, appeared as a feature article in People Magazine, and is the subject of an upcoming Hollywood movie, which is still in the works. Emily's face graced the 1997 Great American Meat-Out poster distributed to thousands of volunteers. She was the campaign's first ever "poster cow." The Great American Meat-Out is coordinated nationally by FARM, the Farm Animal Reform Movement, a non-profit public interest organization formed in 1981 to promote planetary health through plant based eating.

Emily, as an Ambassador for barnyard animals, never shied from cameras and was always ready to let interviewers know that behind her bright beautiful expression was a mind, a personality, and a spirit that exuded optimism for the day in the future when the human species that almost butchered her in her youth would become aware of the rights of animals – the right to be free from harm, the right to be unencumbered by humans, and the right to pursue self-interests, and the respect of existence to not be viewed as a commodity for commercial interests.

Emily forged many bonds, gave countless people many stories to tell, and made many connections between human morality and animal compassion.

"[Emily] is very affectionate and has huge eyes that look through you. Some animals have a deep presence, Emily has her wisdom," boasted Emily's adopted mom, Meg Randa.

From her barn and field on the grounds of the Peace Abbey, Emily was always open to receiving visitors and adding inter-species significance to the Pacifist Memorial that Lewis Randa established. The Pacifist Memorial consists of six long brick walls upon which are placed greater than 60 bronze plaques with the names and quotes of women and men who devoted their lives to non-violent social change. It also has prayers of peace from 12 major religions. The quotes are drawn from such notables as Cesar Chavez, Peace Pilgrim, Martin Luther King, Jr. Oscar Romero, Dorothy Day, John Lennon, Gandhi, and Jesus.

Emily was also attentive and loving to the special needs children and young adults of the Life Experience School in Sherborn that Lewis Randa directs.

Visitors to Emily have included among others from around the world and locally, eight Buddhist Nuns from the Keydong Thuk-Che Cho-Ling Nunnery of Tibet. The Nunnery, which has a long history of saving animals from slaughterhouses was founded to pursue fasting and prayers to the deity of compassion for the benefit of the large herds of sheep sent to slaughter in the Keydong Province of Nepal.

People came from around the globe, across the nation, and locally to visit with Emily. Visitors from India came to bless her as a sacred cow and brought her a handmade sacred cow blanket. She was the inspiration for many vegetarian, animal sanctuary, justice, spiritual building, and religious events. She had many friends.

"Emily opened the eyes of thousands of people to the cruel treatment of cows by the dairy industry, and the suffering these animals go through," said Lewis Randa of the Peace Abbey. Then in early March 2003, Emily started loosing weight and her abdomen filled with fluid. Doctors determined that she had cancer. Her treatment would have been experimental and she was getting weaker by the hour.

What perhaps sent her to slaughter at the young and tender age of 2 years old was what caused her death at the young age of 10 years old. Because of the cancer growing in her, she was unable to become pregnant and, therefore, unable to produce milk. Thus she must have been sent to slaughter because she was not deemed profitable to the dairy industry. Eventually, the painful cancer grew and prevented her from her normal functions. There was little that doctors could do for her. As the Peace Abbey community held their hands clenched in wishful prayer for Emily to clear another deadly hurdle, the dreaded words were broadcast:

"Emily – 10 years old; died in her sleep of uterine cancer."

On Sunday March 30, 2003, Emily died peacefully in her sleep, in her stall at the Peace Abbey, surrounded by her farm animal friends in the barn. Emily's body was laid in state, so people could come to say their good-byes and reflect about her life.

Emily was buried in the field behind Gandhi's Statue and the Pacifist Memorial.

Shortly after Emily's burial on April 2, 2003, a memorial ceremony was held by the bereaved Randas at the Peace Abbey. Emily was part of their family. An international community had grown around Emily. The ceremony was open to the world since the world community needed to reflect upon the passing of Emily. Most people could not personally attend because of the travel distance around the globe, and some had commitments they could not break. Emails, letters and telephone calls poured in for Emily expressing condolences and relaying strong emotional ties to her presence in their lives.

At the ceremony, people packed into the Quaker Room of the Peace Abbey and overflowed out the doors to celebrate the life of Emily, and express and share sorrow for her passing. Represented were people from Animal Rights, Animal Welfare, Peace, Vegetarian, Environmental, and Social Justice movements. There were people from the Religious communities, townspeople, people from surrounding towns, people from the Life Experience School that the Randas run, doctors and a host of others.

Meg Randa in reaching out to the community offered the following words in reflecting upon the life of Emily. "We must learn that animals are thinking, feeling creatures with the same will to live that any other creature possesses. She was an ambassador for all animals and her life and story is a testimony to the fact that all life is sacred."

Lewis Randa summarized in his eulogy over Emily that "Emily was more than just a cow. She was, for people who loved her, an important creature who put them in touch with a greater understanding of animals and how humans should treat them. Her eyes would melt your heart and make you appreciate what animals have to offer."

To others Emily has been a role model. Lewis described a woman, struggling to leave an abusive relationship that was resolved after the woman visited Emily. The woman said, "If she can, I can." The woman was so moved by Emily's escape that a few months later she ended the relationship and credited Emily with providing the inspiration for her too, to escape.

One special needs student described how he had been working outside the barn on an icy day, and slipped down a hill and broke his pelvis. Emily mooed and mooed until someone came out and realized that the boy was injured.

Mary Corthell said, "I first met Emily when Kaia was about 8 months old," When Emily would see the baby she would take her big tongue and lap her starting from toe to head and back again. The little girl would laugh with glee. When she turned four, she wanted to be Emily for Halloween, so her Mom made her a black and white Holstein cow costume. She wanted Emily to see her all dressed up. When she walked in front of Emily's paddock, this 1800 lb. cow took her big tongue and licked her from toe to head and back again. The little girl was so happy that Emily liked the costume. The mother had her camera with her, but felt that a picture would never have captured the special moment she had just witnessed.

Miryam Wiley in commentary on the death of Emily wrote from the context of how she and her family suddenly realized that Emily was part of their lives, and as she reflected on how she and her family would miss Emily she said she felt that, "Emily was a barometer of all good things."

Alexandra Santilli said, "We love her and miss her. Emily fought so hard to save herself from slaughter but when her message was sent and her job was done she accepted death peacefully. All animals deserve nothing less.

For Sharlet Ramsland, Emily wasn't just an inspiration to become vegetarian: Ramsland and her son Charlie, 5, opened an animal sanctuary to save other animals from slaughter. "She changed us," Ramsland said, as she fought back tears. "She's very powerful."

Many who attended the memorial for Emily remembered her as an animal with an uncanny ability to touch people's lives.

Kathy Berghorn wrote, "[Emily] you were a living reminder that we are all one. You made no distinctions and reminded us to do the same. You catalyzed a new awareness in people by your presence. One look into your large, luminous brown eyes communicated so much more than words ever could. Who can say how many people felt a new awareness of compassion as they stood quietly with you?"

Evelyn Kimber, President of the Boston Vegetarian Society and principal organizer of the annual Boston Vegetarian Food Festival reflected upon Emily's life thusly, "It was said by others that Emily 'put a face on vegetarianism'. That summarized quite well the value of Emily's story in helping people to identify with an individual animal who saw death and wanted life, just as any of us would. Discussions about farmed animals often refer to numbers in the billions, which can numb the listener to the fact that each one is a living, suffering individual who values life and will do everything in her power to save herself. Beyond that, Emily's personality and charisma made people think hard about what meat really is, where cow's milk comes from, and if a taste for those products possibly justify harming and killing a creature like her."

The passing of Emily was noted in the Wednesday April 2, 2003 Society Section of the Boston Globe where the following commentary appeared, "... Last night Emily was remembered at a memorial service in the Quaker Room at the Peace Abbey. "It's actually been quite beautiful – all the outpourings of support we've received – emails from all over the world," said Lewis Randa who along with Meg runs the Peace Abbey."

A record of Emily's life resides on a table in the foyer of the Guest House at the Peace Abbey. It is filled with pictures, history, commentary, and the following synopsis of her life: Emily Escaped from the Slaughterhouse 11/15/95 Entered the Peace Abbey 12/24/95 Passed on to greener pastures 3/30/03 Buried behind Gandhi's Statue 4/2/03.

The animal rights community is thankful to the Peace Abbey for their understanding that all life is sacred, and for their commitment to the worldwide call for peace amongst humanity, and with animals.

Printed in INCITY WORCESTER TIMES -
October 2, 2003 (Gandhi's Birthday)

Author, vegan and animal rights activist Steve Baer at Emily's Memorial.

The following articles chronicle the journey of an extraordinary bovine that arrived at a small slaughterhouse in Massachusetts nameless and frightened, but determined to stay alive. Following her heroic escape and forty day sojourn in the woods, she was brought to live in sanctuary at The Peace Abbey, a multi-faith center for the study and practice of nonviolence and pacifism located 17 miles west of Boston.

Dozens of journalists and photographers from numerous newspapers and magazines covered her life over a ten year period as she became a local folk hero and legend -- and was viewed by many as a sacred cow. Her story made news around the world and captured the attention of animal lovers who found in her struggle to stay alive reason to question their practice of consuming meat. For many, this hefty-Holstein became their most compelling reason for becoming vegetarian.

The cow's name, as you know, is Emily, and these are the articles written about her. She was an amazing creature that had a wondrous effect on people. She was our bovine bodhisattva.

Meg & Lewis Randa
Sherborn, Massachusetts

11

ESCAPED COW STAYS ON THE MOVE

By Rodney M. Schussler

HOLLISTON Wanted, dead or alive: Emily, a 2-year-old Holstein who has spent five weeks on the lam after hopping a five-foot gate out of the building at Arena's Slaughterhouse just hours before she was to be turned into hamburger.

Using sheer-wit and bovine insight, the 1,600 pound animal has eluded police and its owners by cleverly remaining in the backwoods along Ash Street, supported by an underground network of fans who have left her hay and other food.

And try as they may, the employees at Arena's have been unable to lure the black and white spotted cow back into captivity.

"This is one of the quickest cows I have ever seen," said one employee, who did not want to be identified as an Emily-sympathizer. "When I saw her jump that gate, I thought she was a reindeer in a cow costume. She knew what was coming."

Emily's story has slowly rippled across town as more and more people have sighted the brave refugee.

She has remained in the woods between Ash Street and the Ashland border; she once wandered into the center of town. She has even been seen among a pack of deer.

Police estimate they have fielded about a dozen reports of Emily sightings and have made contact with the cow a couple of times, but been unable to corral her.

"It's become mission impossible for us. By the time we send someone down there, she's gone," said dispatched Lou Gonzalez. "She's no fool. She knows her fate."

Community support for the animal has slowly grown. Many residents refuse to report sightings. Rumor has it that it was a young relative of slaughterhouse owner Frank Arena who actually gave the cow her name.

"There's no doubt people have been feeding this cow," said Police Chief William McRobert.

He said his officers are instructed to attempt to detain the cow and won't shoot unless Emily threatens the public safety.

"There is no way we're going to shoot that cow in someone's front yard. People would not like that," he said.

Emily spotted in the woods behind the slaughterhouse.
(Photo by Bill Thompson, Middlesex News)

Resident Robert Ahearn said he first saw Emily last week while putting Christmas decorations on his house.

"I heard the crunch in the snow and I thought it was my wife. Then this large cow came around the corner. We were both a bit startled," he said.

"She seemed to be in a bit of a hurry, and left," he said.

A vegetarian, Ahearn said he is rooting for Emily and will do anything to help the refugee.

"If she stopped, I would have fed her," he said. "I'd even buy her if I had a place to keep her."

Neighbor Terrie Rivers was doing the dishes last week when her 10-year old son said he saw a 'cheeseburger' in the yard.

"I didn't know what he was talking about. Then there she was, right outside the yard," Rivers said. "I'm not afraid of cows, but she was big.

Arena has been out of town the past few days, but employers said there's little doubt he wants the cow worth an estimated $500 back.

That may not be so easy, according to Dr. George Saperstein, a veterinarian with the Tufts University School of Veterinary Medicine's farm animal unit in Woodstock, Conn.

If Emily is to be sold for human consumption, he said, she must be killed at the slaughterhouse. She can be sold privately if she's killed away from the slaughterhouse, but must be bled instantly. If she's tranquilized, she can't be used for food for up to three years, depending on the drug used, he said.

He said a Holstein is a hardy animal and would have little problem surviving the cold weather and snow, but would need food - about 40 pounds a day - to live.

"If she's still alive for that long, then she's getting food somewhere. People have to be feeding her," he said. "She can survive off fat for a while, but not that long."

Her fate may soon be sealed. Employee's at Arena's said they have been leaving hay out for the Holstein, and she has been eating it. One employee said they would try to recapture Emily in the next few days.

THEY WANT THAT COW

By Rodney M. Schussler

HOLLISTON Two local men and a Sherborn school are trying to save Emily, the 1,600 pound fugitive Holstein and the town's cause celebre.

The 2-year-old cow took one look inside Arena's slaughterhouse on Ash Street on Nov. 14 and jumped a five-foot gate out of the building, disappearing into the woods. Her bravado, cleverness, and instinctual prowess have kept her alive and free ever since.

Police yesterday fielded dozens of inquiries from people who read about Emily's plight in the Middlesex News. Emily was spotted yesterday afternoon near Ash Street, just a few blocks away from the slaughterhouse.

Experts said today's heavy snow shouldn't harm the spotted black-and-white bovine.

"The snow won't bother them, but the deeper it is, the harder it is for them to forage for food," said Dr. George Saperstein, a veterinarian with the Tufts University School of Veterinary Medicine's farm animal unit in Woodstock, Conn.

Hopkinton resident Ernest Clark, an administrator at Tufts University Dental School, a self-professed animal lover said "Emily has become symbolic."

Sherborn resident Meg Randa, who said she read Emily's story and almost cried. "We are deeply committed to saving the life of a cow so determined to avoid her fate," she said.

Randa, along with her husband Lewis, runs The Peace Abbey and The Life Experience School in Sherborn, a multi-faith facility which serves special needs students. She said the Abbey has a few farm animals and room for more.

She and her husband Lewis, both vegetarians, are so concerned about the fugitive bovine that they plan to trek through the snow today to scout the woods for Emily.

For those interested in saving Emily, there are two complicating factors: she remains hidden and Frank Arena owns her.

Arena did not return a phone call to his home last night and was not at the slaughterhouse most of the day.

Randa said she left a message for Arena.

Then there's catching her. "No one has been able to catch her for five weeks. How are we going to?" said Resident Bob Ahearn."

Hopkinton resident Bob Ahearn stands in the side yard of his home on Ash Street where he found Emily wandering out of the woods. (Photo by Shannon McHugh-Power, Middlesex News)

FAMILY BUYS FUGITIVE COW

Now all they have to do is find her;
$100 reward

By Rodney M. Schussler

HOLLISTON There will be 700 fewer pounds of hamburger on store shelves for Christmas after a group of residents yesterday bought a refugee cow from her owner for $1 and began the tough task of enticing the scared bovine from the woods.

Emily, the 2-year-old Holstein who escaped from the Arena slaughterhouse Nov. 14, remained on the run. One resident even posted a $100 reward for information leading to her capture.

"She's going to have a hard time figuring out the difference between those who are looking for her now and before," said Sherborn resident Meg Randa, the cow's new owner.

The biggest twist in the tale of the 1,600 pound cow was when owner Frank Arena yesterday agreed to sell her to the Randas for $1, well below Emily's $500 market value five weeks ago.

"He said he would sell it because those people wanted it for a good cause," said his daughter Joanne Arena. "We'll even try to help them find Emily and move her."

Joanne Arena said her father was moved by the public support for Emily, who hopped a 5-foot high gate in the slaughterhouse just minutes before she was to be slaughtered.

"If they can take care of her, they can have her," she said.

Yesterday's developments mean Emily, once destined for the meat grinder will live a free life with a horse and two goats at a Sherborn farm- if she is caught.

"We spent hours in the woods and left hay everywhere," Lewis Randa said. "We saw where she had been, but were unable to find her. We'll be out there again today and every day until we bring her in."

Peter Arena said Emily had been nibbling at the food, but he was unable to capture her. "It's not going to be easy," he said.

Clark has posted the reward, hoping it will prompt neighborhood residents to be on the lookout for the spotted black-and-white cow.

"It's motivation for people to get out there and look for this cow," he said.

The Arena family has agreed to transport Emily to Sherborn when she is caught. There, she will join a horse, two goats, and other animals on a farm at the Life Experience School for special needs students.

"She will be a mascot for the school, for the kids and for the movement," said Lewis Randa, a vegetarian.

He also expressed gratitude to the Arena family for their help. "They didn't have to do any of this. They bent over backwards to make this work."

Joanne Arena (daughter of Frank Arena) hands over the bill of sale for Emily the Cow to 8 year old Michael Randa as 6 year old Abbey, Meg and Lewis Randa watch. The Randa family paid one dollar for the cow at the Arena slaughterhouse parking lot. (Photo by Ed Hopfmann, Middlesex News)

COW ON THE LAM

Cowboys offer new owners advice for reining in Emily

By Rodney M. Schussler

HOLLISTON   Meg Randa was becoming a bit discouraged.

It had been more than a day since she and her husband Lewis had bought Emily, a 2-year-old Holstein, from a local slaughterhouse, saving the animal from a certain fate at the butcher's knife and in the meat grinder.

Sitting in her car yesterday afternoon on Ash Street, Randa was still waiting for her first glimpse of the determined animal who had jumped a 5-foot gate at the Arena Slaughterhouse Nov. 14 and had been in hiding ever since.

Suddenly, the 1,600 pound cow emerged from the woods and nibbled on a stack of hay.

"There she was," Randa recalled. "I finally saw her. It was exhilarating."

As Randa approached, Emily quickly disappeared into the thick and snowy woods. Randa followed her tracks and "lots of fresh manure" to a clearing.

"I looked around and didn't see her. Then I turned and there she was. I was looking her in the eye. She was a lot bigger than I thought. I thought she was a bull and was going to knock me down," Randa said.

The Randas and Emily spent about four hours together yesterday, just getting to know each other.

"Eventually she sniffed my hand and ate from a bucket (of grain) Lewis was holding. I really believe she knows we're there to help. Just looking her in the eye was amazing. I think she's ready to come in," said Randa.

Getting Emily "in" may be easier said than done. The cow remains in the woods between Ash Street and the Ashland border.

"After seeing her today, we didn't know what to do," she said.

To that end, livestock experts from across the nation yesterday offered tried and true methods they use when a cow isn't cooperative.

Vermont dairy farmer Frances Howrigan said when he loses a heifer he gets on a horse, gets a herding dog and tracks the missing animal. Then he runs it back into captivity.

"Or I'd run out a few older cows and some hay and the missing one usually comes in. Both those usually work pretty well," he said.

"Well, we don't have a herding dog," Meg Randa said. "If anybody has one, we'd love to use it."

"I typically saddle a horse and go looking," said Bill Runner, a herder and inspector for the Wyoming Livestock Association. "That's the quickest way to find the animal. I suggest they hire a horse and look."

When Runner finds the wayward cow, he lassos it and quickly ties it to a tree. "I'm a 180-pound man and a 1,600 pound cow would take me right out."

Montana state veterinarian Clarence Siroky suggested the Randas build a trap using metal railings and wood. He said using a rope is a better alternative, but it's not easy. "I'm not sure anyone there is big enough to hold onto it."

Dr. George Saperstein, a veterinarian with the Tufts University School of Veterinary Medicine's farm animal unit in Woodstock, Conn., suggested luring the animal into a trailer.

Randa said that is probably the most feasible solution, but the family still lacks a trailer. "We need some help," she said.

"We'll be out there all day (today) and we'll keep going until we get her," she said.

WE ASKED

Should Emily be turned over to the Randas or turned into hamburger?

READERS SAY FREE EMILY

Not the only desperate animal
I'm glad that Emily is going to get a chance at a second life, and I hope everybody who is moved by her story will try to do something to make life better for another animal, perhaps become a vegetarian, adopt a pet from a local shelter, or even make a donation to a local shelter. Emily's not the only desperate animal out there.
-no initials

Cow Comfort
Keep running Emily the Cow! If you come by my house, I'll feed you. I don't eat meat, so I'd rather see you alive.
- P.A.S., Holliston

Run Emily, Run
In response to your article "Escaped cow stays on the move," I was absolutely horrified to think that this was written as some sort of joke- - "Wanted: Dead or Alive" and "Escaped just hours before she was turned into a hamburger." I am simply outraged. I only hope someone who can care for this poor animal will come forward and purchase this poor animal for a mere $500, which is the value of this animal in the eyes of butchers. Shame on you all. Run Emily, run"
- L.Z., Holliston

Burger
I think the cow should be turned into hamburger. - R.O.B

Make it a Double
I'm up for hamburger. D.W., Hopkinton

Helping a Helpless Animal
Of course Emily should be turned over to the Randas, never turned into hamburger. Emily is a special animal and has to be saved and loved. It shows you the compassion of most people: They would go to the ends of the earth and back to help a helpless animal. God love them. It's truly in the spirit of Christmas. - J.S., Ashland

Keep her safe

I think Emily should not be turned into hamburger. Obviously since she ran away she doesn't want to be turned into hamburger. I think she should be turned over to someone who will take care of her and keep her safe.

- R.H., Hopkinton

'Tis the Season

Regarding Emily the hurdling Holstein: It's important to remember that in this Christmas season, that is was the breath of cattle and oxen that kept the Christ child warm in the manger.

- M.S., Natick

Find her, keep her

I think Emily should be saved and not turned into hamburger because it's Christmastime and she's running for her life. I think whoever finds her should give her to the Randas.

-- no initials

To the good life

I think Emily the cow should definitely be turned over to the Randa family and live a good life

-- C.B., Holliston

Gives up Meat

I think Emily should definitely be turned over to the Randas. Now I'm going to give up all red meat. I think about the plight of cows, and I think it will be a lot better for them and a lot better for me.

-- B.L., Marlborough

Anti-Burger

I surely hope they get hold of Emily the Cow before she gets hurt. She should be turned over to the Randas, not into hamburger.

-- C.H., Hopkinton

Good Neighborhood
The Randas should definitely get Emily. They'll give her wonderful care and a beautiful home in pastoral Sherborn.
--B.S., Holliston

Smart Cow
Any cow that's smart enough to jump over a fence doesn't deserve to be turned into hamburger. I love cows anyway and I definitely wouldn't want anything to happen to Emily.
-- A.L., Franklin

Go Randas
Of course Emily the Cow should be turned over to the Randas. Hooray for them and Hooray for her.
-- A.P., Acton

No Burger
Emily should definitely not be turned into a hamburger.
-- L.J., Marlborough

Wholeheartedly
I agree wholeheartedly with Emily being given to the Randas.
M.F., Framingham

Heartwarming
What a wonderful, wonderful gesture on the part of the Arena Family turning over Emily to the Life Center. Emily's need to escape shows her intelligence, and I hope they find her soon. It's a heartwarming story for Christmas and is just so wonderful. Thank you for letting all of us know about this.
-- M.S., Hopkinton

Vegetarian
I definitely think Emily should be saved by the Randas, and not turned into hamburger. I am a vegetarian, and myself and many others in Southborough wish her the very best and hope that she can be found.
-- K.F., Southbourough

Thanks, News

I was delighted to see that the News did a story on Emily and the Randa family. I certainly hope that they find her: I think that she'll be a wonderful addition to the Peace Abbey and Life Experience School. And I hope that you'll do a story on the Abbey's Life Experience School, which is an absolutely wonderful place. You'll really see what compassion is about.

-- R.D., Framingham

Too Late

I think the Randas should be able to keep Emily because now that they've paid $1 for her, she's legally theirs. The slaughterhouse has had five or so weeks to catch her, and now it's the Randas turn to try.

-- S.R., Natick

Turn her over

Emily should be turned over to the Randas.

-- F.R.

Love Story

Emily should definitely be turned over to the Randas. I know them very well and she will have a wonderful home. This would make everyone happy.

---R.S., Sherborn

Some Cow

There's no question that Emily should be given to the Randas. I'm still waiting for you guys to report that Charlotte has spun a web high in the rafters of Arena's barn that reads "some cow".

-- M.R., Marlborough

A Fighter

Emily the cow should not be turned into hamburger. She fought long and hard to save her life. Let her live. Let her enjoy the rest of her life.

-- F.L.S., Northborough

EMILY THE COW MEETS THE PRESS

By Rodney M. Schussler

HOPKINTON   I have met Emily, and she is big.

After days of chronicling Emily's escape, flight, hiding, near-death and planned rescue, I felt as though I had become one with the 1,600 pound female.

Yesterday, I actually came face-to-snout with the 2-year-old cow, and had the first-date jitters. She was beautiful, black and white, clean and regal. But big.

It's hard to imagine the size of a 1,600 pound animal, but suffice it to say it is very big. She stood over 5 feet tall and about 7 feet long, sort of a large rectangle.

When I approached Emily, Meg and Lewis Randa of Sherborn, Emily's new owners were feeding Emily hay and grain. They were less than a foot away as the animal munched.

As I stomped through the snow, the alert animal watched me. It was like the feeling you get when you're being checked out in a bar: the eyes probe; you look down and keep moving.

By the time I got within a foot of Emily, she was a bit leery, moving backward slowly, munching on hay after a five-week diet of frozen leaves and chestnuts. But I could tell she knew who I was -- the Romeo who had rescued her from the meat grinder.

I finally moved within inches of her, posed for a few photos and stretched out my arm. Then she made a weird grunting noise and backed up.

Whoa. A little alarm in my head reminded me that when staring at a 1,600 pound animal who just made a weird sound, you should freeze. I did. Then she calmed down and kept eating. I said thanks for the memories and left.

Emily, if you haven't heard by now, is the Holstein who took one glimpse at the Arena slaughterhouse on Nov. 14 and hopped a 5-foot gate out of the building. Looking at her yesterday, she looked as if she could walk through such a gate, but not hop it. Yet some animals certain to meet their doom develop a keen sense of reality and exhibit super animal powers.

Since her escape, she has spent most of her time in the woods along Ash Street. She made her way uptown once, blocking traffic in the center for a minute. Mainly she was in the woods, occasionally venturing through a yard looking for some food.

After hearing a school official jokingly tell Emily's tale last week, the reporter in me thought "Great story. Front page. Excellent."

Four front-page stories later, I'm still riding the wave: great animal emotion during the warm and fuzzy holiday season.

For the record, I'm a vegetarian. I'm not sure what its worth, but I'll put it on the table. I'm also a reporter and can sense a great story.

Meg and Lewis Randa reach out to Emily in clearing near slaughterhouse as they offer grain and water to the runaway heifer in an effort to bring her to live at the Peace Abbey. (Photo by Stephen Tackeff, Middlesex News)

Upon reading the first installment of Emily's plight Tuesday, Ernest Clark and Bob Ahearn starting trying to figure out how to save Emily from her fate as an ingredient to Christmas Day stuffing.

Enter the Randas, two devout vegetarians who were touched by the tale and immediately phoned in seeking the latest information.

For many people I've spoken to over the course of the week, Emily has become a symbol. Sure, millions of animals are slaughtered for food each year, perpetuating and endless cycle of violence. So what's one cow?

A lot, according to the many carnivores rooting for the refugee animal. To them, she represents the little cow, fighting for her rights and taking matters into her own hands. If a cow outsmarts a few humans, it's news.

The heroes of this tale are the Randas. They volunteered the Sherborn Abbey as the new home for Emily and received the blessings of the Arena family who parted with the cow for a mere buck. Great work, but it was to get harder.

Today, the Randas will spend their third day in the snowy field along Ash Street, feeding Emily hay and grain, gaining her trust, trying to lure her into a trailer so they can haul her to a warm home.

To many, their efforts may seem extreme. One person said to me yesterday, "Do those vegetarians have a life?" Certainly they do. The couple has three children eagerly awaiting Christmas. They have presents to wrap. Neither Meg nor Lewis has slept much in the past few days.

Christmas is always full of warm stories: People helping the less fortunate by buying them gifts, clothes, food, etc.

Emily, destined to have a bolt driven through her head and then be bled to death and transformed into food, is pretty unfortunate, I'd say.

The Randas are just buying her freedom, giving her a new home and feeding her.

What's wrong with that?

(This article appeared in the paper on Christmas Eve, the day Emily was finally caught and brought to The Peace Abbey. She had been on the run for 40 days.)

EMILY THE WAYWARD COW
KEEPS MOO-VING

By Seth Agulnick
Special to the News

HOPKINTON   They coaxed her with comforting words.

They fed her all her favorite foods (grain, mostly).

They even considered drugging her.

But someone forgot to tell Emily, the fugitive cow from Arena Slaughterhouse, that it was time to cooperate.

Despite another day with no success in luring Emily from the Hopkinton woods, the cow's new owners, Meg and Lewis Randa of Sherborn, are refusing to give up hope.

The Randas paid $1 for the elusive bovine earlier this week after reading about her in the Middlesex News. Emily's been on the run since hopping out of the slaughterhouse on Nov. 14th.

Yesterday, they had a friend back up a trailer to the clearing off Ash Street where Emily has allowed the Randa to get close enough to feed her by hand for the last several days.

After stocking the trailer with fresh hey, the Randas hoped the 2-year-old cow would voluntarily end the cat-and-mouse game by climbing aboard.

After all, voluntary is about the only way to get a 1,600 pound Holstein to do much of anything, though observers believe Emily may have lost as much as half her body weight since she's been on the run.

The only progress, however, was when a friend of the Randas managed to get a rope around Emily's neck before she ducked back into the woods, providing some hope that she could eventually be led into the trailer.

But, alas, it was another day with no captured cow. Still, the Randas planned to pitch a tent overnight and keep a look-out today for the cow they expect to be the newest member of their family.

To most people, the idea of spending the days before Christmas tracking down a runaway cow might seem a little strange.

To Meg and Lewis Randa, it makes perfect sense.

And why shouldn't it?

It's almost a natural extension of the lives the Quaker couple has led up to now.

Since 1972, they've run a school in Sherborn for special education students. In 1988, after a visit from Mother Teresa of Calcutta, they set up a Peace Abbey, which they describe as an 'interfaith retreat', next to the school located at the junction of routes 27 and 16.

And just recently, the Randas opened the Greater Boston Vegetarian Resource Center adjacent to the school.

So how does the mission to save Emily fit in?

"It's another spoke in the wheel of compassionate living," Lewis Randa explained.

The couple plans to keep Emily as a symbol for their vegetarian cause, and allow the students at their school to care for the animal. Emily will live with two horses and goat that the Randas already care for.

Sitting under a banner that reads "The Great American Meat - Out," Meg says the logic people use to justify killing animals for food or clothing -- that it's not cruel because the animals don't understand what's happening to them-- is nonsense.

The Randas' friends don't seem the least bit surprised at the couple's latest mission.

"Only Lewis Randa would have a cow that dies of old age. They're not pet animals," said Bill Greaves of Norfolk, who donated the trailer and a lot of his time to Emily's cause. "Knowing Lewis, he'll make a career out of saving cows."

Though Lewis has been known to give his heart for causes, Emily is actually Meg's obsession.

It was mid-October and Meg was on her way to pick tomatoes with her students as part of a food drive for a local homeless shelter when she first drove by Arena slaughterhouse.

She was deeply disturbed to think that animals were being killed so close by, she said. When she saw the newspaper article about Emily, who escaped the slaughterhouse just moments before she was to be killed, something just clicked in Meg's mind.

"I wake up at 5:30 in the morning and my eyes pop open and I think about her out there," Meg said. "Saving Emily isn't going to help every cow... but the fact that she saved her own life, she becomes a symbol."

Four days into the chase, Meg and Lewis believe Emily will be on their farm in time for Christmas.

"I think she's ready to come home," Meg said. "I think she knows we want to help. I think she's had enough of being a wild cow."

EMILY'S HOME FOR CHRISTMAS

By Sean Gardiner

HOPKINTON   Emily the cow, the brazen bovine who jumped a 5-foot gate at the Arena Slaughterhouse, was finally captured yesterday after 40 days on the mooo-ve.

After spending four days trying to corral the black-and-white spotted Holstein, Meg and Lewis Randa and friends tugged, pushed, and pulled Emily out of the cold at exactly 8:35 a.m. on Sunday, December 24th.

"Emily's been caught," Lewis Randa bellowed into a bullhorn immediately after the capture. He also welcomed Ash Street residents, where Emily had roamed, to visit the cow at the Sherborn Peace Abbey.

"I was saying it from the beginning that wouldn't it be wonderful to have Emily home for Christmas," Meg Randa said. "And today was the day. It really makes me feel like this was meant to be."

Lewis Randa said a movie producer has expressed some interest in Emily's story and his wife thinks the Holstein's Christmas story would make a great children's book.

"The Udder Truth," Lewis couldn't help offering as a possible title. "Her story is about the sad reality of how we treat the animals we eat".

Scheduled for slaughter more than a month ago, Emily, who weighed about 1,600 pounds at the time, jumped a gate out of the Arena Slaughterhouse in Hopkinton on Nov. 14 and made her run for freedom.

"Since that time, the bovine escaped capture, living in the woods of Ash Street on a diet of frozen leafs, chestnuts and bales of hay left by an 'underground network' of Hopkinton residents pulling for the cow's survival," Meg Randa said.

Last week when Emily's story hit the Middlesex News' front page, officials at the slaughterhouse gave up efforts to turn Emily into an entree and sold the feisty Holstein to the Randas for a buck.

With classical music filling the air and Christmas decorations, including a stocking full of hay and oats adorning the Peace Abbey in Sherborn, Emily looked content in her new home yesterday. The Abbey is located at the junction of routes 27 & 16.

"She was really shaking before, but she looks a lot calmer now," Meg Randa said as she extended her hand and Emily licked it and mooed. "That was the first kiss I got and that moo made my day."

Today the Randas plan to cook a vegan stew and have Christmas dinner with Emily in the barn.

Meg Randa said her family was forced to put their usual Christmas preparations on hold while trying to save Emily.

"I've been so focused on saving this cow that I've had to put baking cookies and doing other Christmas things on hold," Meg Randa said. "But I told my kids that this will be the Christmas we'll remember for the rest of our lives. This is what Christmas is all about.

After 40 days in the woods, Emily is pushed into stock trailer by Lewis Randa, Amy & David Moore and Bill Greaves. Bill Greaves supplied his trailer and expertise in the capture of Emily. (Photo by Stephen Tackeff, Middlesex News)

With a little help from their friends, the Randas were able to capture Emily Sunday morning. (Photo by Stephen Tackeff, Middlesex News)

It's not about the presents or thinking about ourselves. It's about helping other creatures."

Like the horses, goats, rabbits, and dogs at the Rte. 27 Abbey farm, Emily will get to teach special needs children how to care for animals and inspire visitors to give up eating meat.

Lewis Randa, who as a vegetarian, is ethically opposed not only to the practice of eating animals but also to the consumption of all dairy products, said he hopes Emily becomes the symbol of the 'vegetarian movement'.

Then, he added striking a more serious note, "Emily will open the eyes of thousands of people to the cruel treatment by the dairy industry and the suffering these animals go through."

Randa explained that cows are artificially inseminated to have babies so they can produce milk, and then the male babies are taken away and killed for veal at a young age. The mother cows are then milked for six to eight months, then re-impregnated, and ultimately,

*Lewis Randa announces to community that Emily has
been rescued and invites everyone to The Peace Abbey to
celebrate. (Photo by Stephen Tackeff, Middlesex News)*

when their milk production decreases with age, they are sent to the
slaughterhouse.

"They give us milk for our children and then we turn around and
kill and eat them. How wrong is that?" he said.

"Emily is safe and sound now, but the 40 days she spent running
for her life in Hopkinton cost her about 500 pounds," Meg Randa said.
The Randas plan on having a veterinarian look at her the day after
Christmas and then start beefing her up, so to speak.

BREAKING BREAD WITH A BOVINE

By Steve LeBlanc

SHERBORN   The Randa family had cow for Christmas dinner. Emily the cow, that is.

That brave-hearted bovine, who late last month cheated death by leaping a five-foot slaughterhouse gate and disappearing into the woods of Ash Street in Hopkinton, was the guest of honor at the Randa's holiday table yesterday.

The five members of the family, who last week adopted Emily to prevent her imminent demise, were so taken with their new addition that they decided to relocate their dinner feast to the barn currently serving as Emily's new home.

Meg Randa said her family, who are strict vegetarians, packed up a meal of vegetable stew, rice, grilled tofu and fresh Italian bread and set up a table near Emily's stall.

Emily, forced to forage for food during her flight from freedom, seemed particularly interested in the bread.

"I put my hand out with a piece of bread and her tongue came out and she ate it. If there was a chair handy, she would have pulled it up and sat down with us, "Meg Randa said.

"I guess we broke bread with the cow," she added.

The outing was especially fun for Meg and Lewis Randa's three children -- Christopher, 12, Mikey, 8, and Abbey, 6. Even the fondest affections couldn't withstand yesterday's freezing temperatures indefinitely. After an hour or so, the family moved back inside, leaving one contented cow behind.

"She looked very peaceful all curled up," Meg Randa said.

Emily captured the imagination of the area after she broke free of Hopkinton's Arena Slaughterhouse on Nov. 14. During her weeks on

Emily safe in her stall at The Peace Abbey in Sherborn. She arrived on Christmas Eve and is the largest and most celebrated Christmas present to arrive at the Abbey ever! (Photo by Stephen Tackeff, Middlesex News)

Emily is safe and warm in her new stall with welcome signs from supporters and friends. (Photo by Lewis Randa)

the lam, Emily was occasionally spotted, but continually eluded capture.

"Emily may have lost hundreds of pounds during her adventure," said Meg Randa, who's hoping to return Emily to her former robust figure.

"She is bony and thin. You can see her ribs," she said.

The family is slowly trying to get her to eat the grains she needs to bring her weight back to normal.

CRAFTY EMILY MOO-VES RIGHT IN WITH SHERBORN CLAN

By Mark Mueller

SHERBORN Life is good for Emily the cow.

Once a hunted escapee from a Hopkinton slaughterhouse, the lumbering 1,600 pound animal was the guest of honor yesterday at a Christmas dinner cooked up by her new owners. Meat wasn't on the menu.

"This has been the most unique Christmas," said Meg Randa of Sherborn, who spearheaded the drive to save Emily from the butcher's cleaver. "To bring her home for Christmas is just a dream come true."

Even Santa came to welcome Emily to the Peace Abbey. (Photo by Meg Randa)

Emily looks out at Gandhi statue her first day in sanctuary. (Photo by Lewis Randa)

Smacking her prodigious gums on warm bran mash laced with molasses and surrounded by animal friends – the Randas also care for two horses, a goat, rabbits and a couple of dogs – Emily was in cow heaven.

But it wasn't always so.

Destined to become hamburger, Emily last month managed to heave her tremendous bulk over a 5-foot gate out of the Arena Slaughterhouse in Hopkinton.

Hunted by police and slaughterhouse employees, the calculating cow lay low in the woods of Hopkinton for over five weeks, hanging around with deer and eking out an existence on winter shrubs and the generosity of strangers.

"There was an underground network of people who'd been leaving hay out for her," Randa said.

Randa, her husband Lewis and their three children -- vegetarians and animal lovers -- soon joined the search in hopes of adopting the slippery heifer.

They finally spotted Emily on Friday, and Randa, with the help of friends, coaxed the cow to give up peacefully on Sunday morning, Christmas Eve day.

Now she's found a home, safe forever from a date with a meat hook. Randa says the slaughterhouse's owner agreed to sell Emily for a mere $1, providing what she calls the season's best Christmas present.

Even with the happy ending, Hopkinton might not have heard the last of Emily, who, with one leap over a fence, might now make the leap to the silver screen.

"We just got contacted by a movie producer about Emily," Randa said. "We might have a star on our hands."

LIFE IS NO LONGER AT STAKE FOR EMILY

Associated Press

SHERBORN   Emily, a cow that fled her fate at a slaughterhouse, is out of the woods.

The cow stole the hearts of residents here last month when she hauled her 1,600 pound frame over a gate, off a dock and out of the building and fled into the woods to escape the Arena slaughterhouse in neighboring Hopkinton.

Her days on the lam ended on Christmas Eve when she was hauled into a trailer and off to live on a small farm behind the Peace Abbey.

"We have been hoping she would just follow a bucket of grain into the trailer," said Meg Randa, hours after her husband, Lewis, and a few friends managed to reel in the hesitant heifer.

In the six weeks since her escape, Emily had eluded police, slaughterhouse workers and animal control officers. She lived mostly off the land, but occasionally ate hay left on porches by sympathetic townsfolk.

Then, on Saturday, one of the Randa's friends managed to get a rope looped around the fugitive cow's neck. That set the stage for yesterday's roundup in a Hopkinton field.

Lewis Randa tied a longer lead to the end of the rope, fed it through the back of the trailer, and with a friend's help, pulled.

"She took off," his wife said. "They held on hard enough and pulled her back and reeled her in, pulled her back, reeled her in. She put up quite a fight, frightened, as she had narrowly escaped death."

But Emily had little to fear from the Randas, who paid the slaughterhouse $1 to let them catch the cow and give her a new home at their Peace Abbey's Life Experience School for special needs children.

The Randas enjoyed a vegetarian Christmas dinner out in the barn, surrounded by Emily and the rest of the family -- two horses, a goat, several rabbits, cats and dogs.

As for Emily's future, the Randas hope she becomes a 'spokescow' against eating meat. As Lewis Randa put it: "People can either listen to Emily and give up eating meat, or they can listen to their cardiologist in the future."

Close call ... thin and mellow, Emily stands in her new stall having barely escaped being returned to the slaughterhouse. (Photo by Stephen Tackeff, Middlesex News)

Emily the cow's story revives meat debate

By Rodney M. Schussler

The efforts of a Sherborn family is vegetarians to find, rescue and adopt an escaped steer in Hopkinton last week highlighted a sensitive topic stirring to more and more dinner tables and restaurants: How much meat should we eat, if any?

Reams of information and stores of opinions on both sides of the topic don't make reaching a documentary easier.

Neither carnivores nor vegetarians can provide definitive data to show people who live otherwise why they should or shouldn't eat poultry, beef, pork or fish.

For some, meat eating is a factor in low-fat diets trumpeted by the media and medical establishment. But for most, becoming a vegetarian is more than a matter of personal health.

"What the whole vegetarian argument comes down to is a moral issue which many people are facing more and more. It's up to each person to make their own moral decision, and it's not easy," said R. Glenn Brown, a professor of food sciences at the University of Massachusetts at Amherst.

MEAT PAGE 2A

A meaty issue

- 13 million vegetarians in the U.S.
- 1 million become vegetarians yearly.
- 40% of these people are under age 17.
- A 70-year-old person will eat 5,000 animals in a lifetime.
- 7.7 billion animals are slaughtered each year in the U.S.
- 7 billion are chickens, 240 million are turkeys.

Average per capita consumption of meat in the U.S. in 1995

EMILY THE COW'S STORY REVIVES MEAT DEBATE

By Rodney M. Schussler

The efforts of a Sherborn family of vegetarians to find, rescue, and adopt an escaped cow in Hopkinton last week highlighted a sensitive topic coming to more and more dinner tables and restaurants: How much meat should we eat, if any?

Reams of information and scores of images on both sides of the topic don't make reaching a decision any easier.

Neither carnivores nor vegetarians can provide definitive data to show people who feel otherwise why they should or shouldn't eat poultry, beef, pork or fish.

For many, meat eating is a factor in low-fat diets trumpeted by the media and medical establishment. But, for most, becoming a vegetarian is more than a matter of personal health.

"What the whole vegetarian argument comes down to is a moral issue which many people are facing more and more. It's up to each person to make their own moral decision, and it's not easy," said R. Glenn Brown, a professor of food sciences at the University of Massachusetts at Amherst, former farmer and meat eater.

Meat supporters claim that meat, in moderation, is no more unhealthy than French fries, ice cream, or eggplant parmesan. They say animals were put on Earth to serve humans and the meat industry provides a living for millions of Americans.

Vegetarians say meat is unhealthy and the leading cause of obesity, cancer and heart disease. They claim meat is loaded with pesticide residue from the grain that animals raised for food consume. They also say the land used to grow animal feed could be used more productively to feed starving humans.

Tangled into all those arguments is the question: is it morally acceptable to kill another living creature for food?

"We don't need to eat animal products to survive and be healthy," said Tracy Reiman, coordinator of the vegetarian campaign for the Washington-based People for the Ethical Treatment of Animals.

"Meat, in moderation, is one of the most integral parts of our diet and is needed for survival," said Bruce Berven, a vice president with the Cattleman's Beef Promotion and Research Board in Englewood, Colorado.

A prime argument of those against meat eating is the harsh treatment of animals used for food.

"What happens to these animals before they are killed is simply not right," Reiman said. For example, she said, pigs and chickens are raised in dark warehouses, stacked on top of each other in small cages.

The meat industry, acknowledging that some animals raised for food lead lives that would not be fit for humans, say it's part of doing business, making a living and feeding people.

Which brings us to the story of Emily, a 2 year-old Holstein who escaped from the Arena Slaughterhouse in Hopkinton last month.

More than 20 people called the Middlesex News supporting the efforts of the Randa family to adopt Emily, destined to be made into hamburger for local stores and restaurants.

Yet an estimated 7.7 billion animals will be slaughtered for human consumption in the United States this year, according to meat industry statistics.

As symbolic as Emily has become, she is a mere drop in the bucket. PETA estimates an average American consumes 1,000 animals in a 70-year lifespan, an average of 14.3 a year. The meat industry says the average American will eat 233 pounds of meat this year, including 124 pounds of beef.

Red meat consumption has fallen from 136 pounds per person in 1980, a fact Berven attributes to what he considers "false" health risks. "All those health issues can be dispelled. Beef fits into a healthy, balanced diet."

Brown, the UMass professor, agrees, adding that the life expectancy of a vegetarian is negligible when compared to a carnivore. "You can't run around on pasta alone."

Reiman concedes that point, but, she says, "Regardless of lifespan, a vegetarian diet allows you to have a healthier life while you live."

The health risks and talk of cholesterol is one of the keys reasons there are, PETA says, more than 15 million American vegetarians, a number the group says is growing by one million per year.

Besides issues of health and cruelty, the fact remains that the meat industry produces money and jobs. A lot of money and jobs.

Brown estimates that the industry makes about 60 percent of the total agricultural sector of the economy when you factor in the production of silage, the food that animals eat. That would make it a $100 billion a year industry.

With land suited for farming becoming precious, Brown said, hillsides and cold weather areas can still be used to graze livestock. "It's a way people make a living on that land."

Berven said the beef industry also powers the farm economy by buying grain which is not safe for human consumption due to spoilage or exposure to the elements.

Reiman argues that if food priorities are shifted to the grain-based vegetarian diet, the money would still be made, but in a different way.

With powerful issues such as food, money and morals in the mix, arguments of meat eating vs. vegetarianism won't likely go away in the coming years, and will probably escalate.

And Emily, the 1,600 pound Holstein who will live the remainder of her expected 12-17 year lifespan on a spacious farm, will be used as a symbol in the fight: Her caretakers plan to make her the mascot of the state's vegetarian resource center which is at the Peace Abbey.

"Hopefully, people will take one look at her and convert," said Lewis Randa.

FROM MEAT GRINDER TO STARDOM

*Hollywood's calling Emily as
fans flock to her side*

By Rodney M. Schussler

SHERBORN Just a week after being spared from the meat grinder, Emily the cow is holding court in her stall, fielding calls from Hollywood as dozens of fans paid homage.

"She has become a celebrity. There's no doubt about it," said Meg Randa, who along with her husband Lewis, bought Emily from a Hopkinton slaughterhouse last week for $1. "And the funny thing is she seems to love every minute of it. She is drawn to people like you can't believe."

In the past three days, Emily, who has achieved heroine status since she ran way from Arena Slaughterhouse in mid-November and hid in the woods, has posed for photos in several newspapers and been featured in a national Associated Press story. She has also been on CBS and NBC evening news as well as talk radio.

"We're going to need a stylist for her pretty soon," joked Meg Randa as she played with a little tuft of hair which has become Emily's trademark cowlick.

The more people hear of Emily's tale of bravery, cunning, instinct and wit, the more they want to know. Following WBZ-TV new reporter Bill Shields' report on Emily Tuesday, anchor Uma Pemmaraju proclaimed: "I love that story!"

Boston political satirist Barry Crimmins sent the Middlesex News a fax informing reporters and editors he would be "bivouacking with the bovine as he prepares for his annual year-in-review show" at Passim Coffeehouse in Cambridge tomorrow.

*Meg Randa concentrating on her interview with Emily
for FOX News. (Photo by Lewis Randa)*

"This afternoon, I contemplated the prospects for the 1996 presidential race and I must say that I am looking forward to returning to Emily's stall," Crimmins' fax said.

The Randas' phone has barely stopped ringing since they brought Emily to safety from the Hopkinton woods on Christmas Eve. The visitors continue to flock to the Peace Abbey where Emily now lives.

Lewis Randa is sending copies of stories to People magazine, hoping to generate even more interest for the vegetarian cause, which Emily has come to represent.

"We saw a lot of potential here for Emily to become the symbol of compassionate food choices," he said.

Meg Randa is writing a children's book and is seeking an illustrator. There may even be an Emily line of veggie burgers someday.

Then there's Hollywood. The Randas have been contacted by a couple of Los Angeles movie production companies and are expecting more inquiries as the story gains more national attention.

One Boston-based movie producer/director said Emily's story may indeed have big screen potential and it's promising that several producers have already called.

"This sounds like movie-of-the week potential to me, "said Steve Bennett, a co-owner of Iron Fist Motion Pictures. "As the story gets more exposure, more people will probably express interest. And as word gets out that someone has expressed interest, then more producers will express interest.

The process of getting from reality to Hollywood is simple, he said. Either a producer or a writer buys the rights to Emily's story, and then she's on her way.

"Selling the rights is the hardest part," he said.

Even if Emily never makes it as a screen star, she has legions of local fans that are making pilgrimages to see her.

Yesterday, Gloria Welch of Framingham and Sally Larnis of Ashland visited Emily after following the Holstein's story in the Middlesex News.

Welch collected all the stories for a friend and former Hopkinton resident who now resides on the West Coast.

"I wanted to end the story by saying, 'Guess what? I met her,'" she joked.

Lewis Randa said he has been surprised by the enormous public interest Emily has generated.

"I have been fascinated by this story ever since the first day," Welch said as she patted Emily's large head. "She's so beautiful."

"Forget about the cow who jumped over the moon," Larnis said as she fed Emily some grain. "This is the cow who jumped over the fence."

EMILY THE COW GIVES 'HOOFERS' HUNGER PANGS

Carolyn Fretz, Regional Editor

I've been a carnivore extraordinaire for most of the years since I've had teeth.

Broiled, grilled, stir-fried. Bring it on, and pass the Worcestershire, please.

But now I have to reconsider.

Filet-mignon. Oooooh, how divine. Or is it?

Cheeseburger. Cheeseburger. Always a safe bet from an unfamiliar menu, but now I'm not so sure.

And steak tartar? I don't think so. Not anymore.

Why?

You know why.

It's Emily - that fence-hopping heifer from Hopkinton.

Emily leaped over a 5-foot corral rail at the Arena Slaughterhouse Nov. 14 - cheating death just minutes before she was scheduled to be butchered.

Forty days and countless adventures later the fugitive bovine met her true density.

She became a folk hero.

She was spotted grazing in the woods with a herd of deer, wandering down Main Street like the moose from Northern Exposure, and feeding in the backyards of residents who learned of her plight and formed a kind of Underground Railroad for the runaway Holstein- leaving grain and hay out for her.

Middlesex News reporter Rodney Schussler heard the tale, put it in the paper and soon Emily wasn't just a local celebrity- she was a 1,600 pound media darling.

Emily with young Gabe looking for attention. (Photo by Meg Randa)

I'm sure I wasn't the only reader to start rethinking what she thought she knew about cows.

A friend who kept cows in Oregon once told me he sometimes used a 4-by-4 to get their attention when he needed to load them into a trailer. Even then, he said, they were very slow to respond.

It was the kind of story that might make you wonder, even if only momentarily, if cows weren't some sort of semi-ambulatory vegetable like eggplant, except they walk.

Wonder no more.

Emily's antics endowed her with more personality, complexity and mystery than many of the two-footers who receive press attention.

Why did it even occur to her to jump the gate? After all, Emily is a cow, not a cheetah or a stallion. Cows just are not the "Born Free" type. Until now, of course. What business did she have downtown on Main Street?

And what about the deer she was seen with? Were they the provocateurs behind the escape? Had they been whispering to Emily from the woods under the cold November moon?

Naturally saviors, now known as Friends of Emily, came forward. Meg and Lewis offered the 2-year-old heifer a home on the farm that adjoins the Peace Abbey and their school for children with special needs. And the Arena family was gracious enough to sell $500 of hamburger-on-the-hoof to the Randas for a mere $1.

Throughout the saga the newsroom telephone lines have been busy with calls from people wanting to know the latest and wanting to help.

And whose heart doesn't go out to a creature so determined to stay alive and to stay free whatever the cost?

We all have a few corrals we dream about leaping, but probably never will.

We all want to think we could run wild and live dangerously.

But we don't have to.

Emily did it for us.

Until Christmas Eve when she came out of the woods, walked up a trailer ramp and went peacefully to her new home in Sherborn.

I went to see Emily a couple days later. The wild one was busy chewing her way through her daily, 40 pound allotment of feed and hay.

She paused long enough to let me rub her neck and to let me know exactly what spot on her enormous head she wanted scratched, thank you.

She seemed alert and content in her toasty stall. And the round, waxy, meat inspector's sticker was starting to wear off her hindquarters.

That's how close this interesting animal came to living and dying in anonymity.

Pass the tofu, please.

FUNNYMAN A FRIEND OF EMILY
Bivouacking with the Bovine

By Rodney M. Schussler

SHERBORN   In his own twisted world, political satirist Barry Crimmins sees great emotional drama in the story of Emily the cow. And some great material.

"I'm going to milk this for everything its worth," he said yesterday as he prepared for one of two year-end shows at Cambridge's Club Passim last night and tonight.

A vegetarian and recipient of the 1994 Courage of Conscience award from the Peace Abbey, Crimmins said he was planning to visit the Abbey and just say hello until he heard Emily's story.

"First Mother Teresa, then Emily. This place attracts world-class beings," he said.

He decided to stay and, never modest, issued press releases Wednesday saying he was "bivouacking with the bovine."

But a small spat occurred and the duo has decided separate bedding is best.

"Emily thought it was be easier for me to prepare for my show inside because there is too much press and well-wishers coming through the barn," he said.

But he did clean her stall, which he said is "better than dealing with politicians. The stench is better."

His initial encounter with the 2-year-old Holstein was love at first sight. "She licked me on the forehead and took a couple layers of epidermis off."

Emily, who jumped a fence to escape the throes of death and was since adopted by the Randa family, has given him some good stuff for his show.

"Name anyone else you know who lost 500 pounds during the holidays," he said, testing one of his new jokes.

Now residing in Cleveland, which he said he could never do without the Internet, Crimmins came back to Boston, where he resided for many years, for his annual year-in-review show.

He said he has some great new material and will also, for the first time, tell sentimental stories from his youth.

"The statue of limitations on most of the stuff I did has expired," he said.

Political satirist Barry Crimmins speaks about his friendship with Emily who he hangs out with when he is performing in the Boston area. (Photo by Meg Randa)

The 1996 presidential election also gives him great inspiration- and sadness.

"The worst problem with that is: one of those guys is going to win," he said.

But he enjoys hanging out with Emily and said he was deeply touched by her tale and will put out a bucket at his shows to raise money to feed the cow.

"Once again these people at the Peace Abbey have established that having a good conscience and doing the right thing can be a lot of fun," he said.

REPORTER:
WHY THE FUSS?
IT'S JUST A COW

by Lucas Mearian

I agree with the soy bean eating, granola types out there, slaughtering Emily the cow for hamburger is a horrible waste. Sirloin steak is far better use.

Let's take a reality break here. It's just a cow.

People have phoned and written to us about their deep concern for the escapee from slaughterhouse row. The press has given the animal folk hero status through syndicated news services. People are taking pictures of it, feeding it, sleeping with it, and now the half-ton Holstein is becoming a bridesmaid for a wedding ceremony at the Peace Abbey in Sherborn.

Hello. Is it me or are these people a few beers short of a six-pack?

The trouble with Emily didn't begin when she jumped the fence at the Arena Slaughter-house. It started when someone gave her a name. That's what prompted an outpouring of reactionary-style compassion.

This happens every time an animal "in need" becomes Lucy, Ralph or Emily. And the outpouring of affection is just as fake this time as every time before.

"Once you give her a name, you can't kill her. That was their mistake," said Edward Rome, of Natick, a chef the past 15 years. "I'm sure in the Philippines they don't kill the family dog either."

As sure as I'm sitting here, dumbfounded by the media frenzy, I'm just as sure all those people who are now vowing to eat lawn clippings and tree bark for the rest of their lives will undoubtedly revert back to good ole' t-bones and New York strip once the hype blows over.

Emily begins to bond with people early on. (Photo by Lewis Randa)

When they do, Chef Rome suggests the best use for Emily is not as a pet, but as a versatile food source.

"Of all the animals that we slaughter, the cow is the most useful. The cow is to us what the buffalo was to the Indians," he said. "We get leather from its hide, gelatin from its hooves, dog toys from its ears, and feed the birds with its suet.

"Now that it's someone's pet, they could make it into a family meal," Rome said. "You could broil, braze, sauté, bake, boil, fricassee, fry, stew or marinate it. You can slice it, dice and grind it. You can eat it raw in steak tartar. We eat all the assorted parts: the liver, heart, tongue and kidneys. Cows are a very versatile animal."

When I think of Emily, I don't get teary-eyed. I get hungry.

I'm not the only one rolling my eyes at this bull-oney.

"I don't think there's anything wrong with showing compassion for the cow, but at least let's get our priorities straight," a colleague said.

I don't doubt that humans can live healthy, happy lives as vegetarians if they choose, but in reality we're omnivores. We'll eat anything and have been for 35 million years or so. I feel a deep obligation to continue that tradition.

Emily is a cow, and like millions of other domesticated animals each year, her lot in life is to be fattened for slaughter so that we can enjoy our Big Macs. Hey, when they become smart enough to avoid capture, then I'll stand up for them. Until then, let's just make sure they get a merciful death -- and lots of onions and mushrooms and peppers with a potato on the side.

Maybe I should've prefaced this by saying I love animals. I do. I've never had the desire to hunt one with a high-caliber rifle that has a 10-power scope atop. That isn't a sport.

But at the same time, I don't deny my nature and I don't pretend to be ignorant of where my food source comes from or act ashamed of it. But vegetarians take heart: studies show you live years longer than us carnivores, which means at 85 you can start calling the shots. Until then, leave my steak alone.

Meg Randa reads some of her favorite vegetarian recipes while Emily reads along to make sure they are meatless and cruelty-free! (Photo by Frank Veronsky of People Magazine)

EMILY'S LESSON IN VEGETARIANISM

By Christof Heinrich

One day she was scheduled to land on your skillet, the next she'd hoofed her way straight into your heart.

Unless you subscribe to the Middlesex News primarily for use as a daily supply of cat litter box liner, you probably know who I'm talking about: Emily the Cow.

That exclusive, warm-nosed, dare I say, intelligent (a term jealously guarded and reserved for a few select creatures whom we do not eat like dogs and cats), bovine who, six weeks ago sensed her imminent grisly fate, and cleared a five-foot metal gate at the Arena Slaughterhouse in Hopkinton

With a leap that literally defied death, Emily cleared a very real physical barrier. She also crossed an invisible and arbitrary psychological wall, becoming, instead of one of several billion faceless animals annual marched to their death in slaughterhouses across the nation, an individual. One animal with, thanks to one of Frank Arena's young nieces, a name. A living being with a brain, a heart, intelligence, capable of feeling pain, and, quite obviously, fear. On the same day slaughterhouse owner Frank Arena handed Emily's $1 bill of sale over to Sherborn residents Meg and Lewis Randa, I suspect many of her fellow dairy cows met a decidedly different fate behind the building's closed doors. This beloved bovine's break for freedom was one-in-a-million.

But the purpose of this column is not to criticize Frank Arena or slaughterhouse owners. They, like the rest of us, are just trying to earn a living. And, though the knife might be in their hands, it really lies in ours.

I am, as you might have guessed, a vegetarian. I took a gradual path to vegetarianism (In fact, because I still do occasionally dabble in

Emily clowning around with Mikey and Chris Randa (Photo by Lewis Randa)

sea-food, I must admit I'm not quite there.) About four years ago, out of concern for my health and our environment, I stopped eating beef, the most energy intensive of all meats. A year-and-a-half ago, after spending a summer riding my bike 4,000 miles across the country with my devoutly vegetarian sister, I dropped all "red" meat from my menu. This past October, I happened upon a book called "Diet for a New America." Written by vegetarian John Robbins - an heir to the Baskin-Robbins ice cream empire who turned down any windfall on philosophical grounds - the book convinced me to drop chicken from my diet as well.

In "Diet for a New America," Robbins argues, quite convincingly, that cows, pigs, and chickens, like dogs, cats are intelligent, feeling beings. He also sheds light on what goes on behind closed doors so many of us are loathe to open or, incredibly (and illogically), whose very existence a sizable number of us choose to ignore altogether.

Our society's treatment of the issues surrounding the consumption of meat is denial on a gargantuan level. "Don't talk to me about how this steak got here, I don't want to know!" say meat eaters.

Is it me, or isn't it strange that the same society which preaches "knowledge is power", (knowledge about what you consume, be it prescription drugs, or a new car, which empowers you with ability to make an intelligent choice) declares demonstratively, " I don't want to know!"?

As longtime border-line vegetarian, I know nothing inspires more passion than a discussion of food choices. To talk about meat (whether I initiate the conversation or not) is to risk an angry verbal barrage. But I sometimes wonder how informed a choice people are making. As a long-time meat eater, I understand the angry responses: I believe most of us, deep down, feel at least somewhat uncomfortable with the consumption of meat and what it entails. Very few of us, though, closely examine our decision to eat it.

We are, Robbins maintains, indoctrinated from the youngest of ages. Meat, we are told by teachers, parents, even "health experts," is essential to our well-being. The ongoing indoctrination (supported by the powerful pork, beef, and fowl industries) is so complete, I believe, that vegetarianism is viewed as border-lining on sacrilege or as unpatriotic.

To choose not to eat meat is to challenge a hallowed pillar of Americanism. It is viewed as elitist, a direct affront to good, old-fashioned American values.

I do not consider myself "elitist" and I am saddened to think some people certainly view me as such because of my personal lifestyle choice. You may also be surprised that I do not wish to push vegetarianism on others. I am simply asking people to make an informed decision on whether to consume meat, to think about how that hamburger reached their plate and where it came from.

I think all Americans would benefit from some simple, potentially heart wrenching, introspection on the repercussions of meat consumption. Afterward, many will decide to continue to eat meat. Some might make an effort to purchase meat from animals raised only under conditions officially sanctioned as humane. Others might choose to reduce their consumption of meat. And a few might decide to stop eating meat altogether. No matter what decision they make, though, it will be an informed choice. And that, I believe, is the most important issue of all.

ALWAYS A BRIDESMAID

Photo by Steven Tackeff

Emily attempts to taste the Bride's flowers during the wedding ceremony of Heather Ralph and groom Gary Tamashian in the barn at The Peace Abbey. Peace Chaplain Dot Walsh officiated with Emily serving as the flower girl, yesterday at the Peace Abbey in Sherborn. Jennifer Ralph, far left, Heather's sister, was maid of honor. Emily didn't catch the bouquet, but may have eaten it.

EMILY BASKS IN THE LIMELIGHT
Vegetarians rally 'round Emily the Cow

By David Traub

SHERBORN   People Magazine may be featuring an animal in its pages sometime soon, since a reporter came to MetroWest yesterday to visit Emily, the region's most famous cow.

"Their writer spent about two hours out here," said Meg Randa, who, with her husband provided sanctuary for the bovine that escaped from the Arena Slaughterhouse and spent 40 days on the lam.

A People photographer also dropped in with "a pretty elaborate lighting system," to be sure to catch Emily's good side.

It should be easier than catching Emily.

The creature eluded capture for over a month in the woods of Hopkinton after jumping a five-foot gate out of the Arena Slaughterhouse. She came in from the cold Christmas Eve.

The Randas, who are vegetarians, have given Emily a home at the Sherborn Peace Abbey.

Since the end of Emily's 40 days in the wilderness, she and the Randas have had more than their share of media attention.

After Lewis Randa spoke about vegetarianism during an appearance on the "Alder On-Line" television program, the show got a number of calls from people interested in going meatless.

"A number of folks said they wanted to commit themselves to the process, the journey of being a vegetarian," Randa said. "It is not something you do overnight, though many do."

And some will do it overnight, tonight.

Over a dozen people came to the Abbey's barn at 12 noon New Year's Day to swear off eating meat.

SONGWRITER PAYS TRIBUTE TO EMILY

By Jeff Gilman

SHERBORN   Emily's flight for life from the Arena Slaughterhouse in Hopkinton captured national headlines and may even become the plot of a movie. Now the story has been put into a song.

Ben Tousley, a songwriter from Jamaica Plain, went to the Peace Abbey, Emily's new home, on Sunday to escape a loud New Year's Eve party being thrown by a neighbor. During the night, he decided to write a song about the 2-year old Holstein's travails.

"It's certainly a story that stirs the imagination," said Tousley. "I was seeking some peace that night. Emily's story just really touched my heart. I said, 'Maybe I'll write a little song.'"

The song was performed for Emily by 30 people gathered at the Peace Abbey to make New Year's resolutions to swear off eating meat.

Tousley describes it as an upbeat song with a celebratory or homecoming theme.

He also says the symbolism of the story fits in perfectly with the Christmas season. He said Emily's plight brought out "the whole significance around Christmas time ... you can appreciate the symbolism."

Lewis Randa of the Peace Abbey, who with his wife secured Emily's safety from Arena for $1, was keeping quiet about any movie deal that might be coming in the near future, but he did say he hoped the song will be a part the upcoming film.

Here's a quick preview of the song appropriately titled "Emily"

Chorus:
Emily (Emily)
We're a family (we're a family)
Of frogs and fish and birds and walking creatures.
Emily (Emily)
We're all Mammaly (we're all mammaly)
And we want to welcome you as our new teacher.

You jumped the fence, you ran for life,
Just when your life would end.
They thought of you as milk and meat
We knew you as our friend.

(Chorus)

For forty days and forty nights,
You hid in the woods,

Ben Tousley sings to Emily and others in the barn during the annual Vegetarian New Year's Resolution Party. Meg Randa sings along with Emily. (Photo by Lewis Randa)

While hunters tried to shoot you down
Your lovers brought you food.

(Chorus)
We brought you here on Christmas Eve
Into this manger stall.
Whoever saves a single life,
It's said they save us all.

(Chorus)
I look into your big brown eyes
And see the light that's there.
In all God's creatures, great and small,
The sacred life we share.

(Ends with chorus)

Cover of tape of musical arrangements
written and performed by Ben Tousley
which features the children's song "Emily".

Letter to the Editor

DON'T EAT YOUR FELLOW ANIMALS

By Jessica Almy

HOPKINTON   Emily the cow probably never thought about more than saving her own life when she escaped from the slaughterhouse on Nov. 14. Surely after being raised as nothing more than a machine for converting grain to milk and flesh, she had little desire to give her life to the humans who had long denied her dignity and freedom, so she grasped the opportunity to escape before she was coldly murdered with her companions.

Little did Emily know she would be on the front page of the local paper day after day or that people from the community would be phoning in to give their opinions on whether or not she deserved to live. Emily is lucky. She has a name, and somehow a community that bites into a burger without giving it a thought has attributed to her feelings and a will to live. How different is it with those cellophane-wrapped packages that barely bleed? They were once living, breathing, sentient creatures with feelings and a will to live, just like Emily.

Make this holiday season a celebration of life: please don't eat your fellow animals.

RECALLING A COW'S STORY

By Huna Rosenfeld

When I first read the story of Emily the Cow, it immediately reminded me of a similar experience I had 45 years ago.

In 1950 I worked with my father as a cattle dealer and butcher on Village Street in Millis. We owned and operated a slaughterhouse that was situated 700 feet behind our house and barn.

On one of our slaughtering days, I drove the cow truck with two cows and a few calves in it to the door of the slaughterhouse. For some now unknown reason, I opened the calf door to look inside and a big Holstein (black and white) cow of about 1,200 pounds stuck its head out of that calf door and started to push through.

I ran back and watched and could not believe what I saw. This cow, snorting and acting completely wild, came out of the calf door, which was only about two feet by two feet in size. No one could believe that it would be possible.

The cow ran off into the woods and despite numerous spottings and attempts to catch it; she was loose and on the lam for three weeks. Finally, a farmer in the area drove it into his barn with some of his own cows.

Unfortunately, my story does not have a happy ending such as Emily's.

I picked up the cow, drove it back to the slaughterhouse, and, as was the destiny of all the cattle in those days, she became hamburger.

Emily with Shoshone and Gabe in the pasture (Photo by Lewis Randa)

REFUSING TO BE COWED BY FAME

Emily the cow being courted by movie producers and glossy magazines after a dramatic escape from a local slaughterhouse

By Philip Maddocks

SHERBORN   Meg Randa, glancing at the unlikely new addition to the barn, can't help but feel it is only appropriate that the newcomer- - a 1,600 pound black and white cow named Emily -- ended up in the barn adjacent to their Life Experience School.

"I have to admit it does seem like destiny," said Randa who, with her husband Lewis, runs the Peace Abbey's Life Experience School. "Lewis and I both believe in synchronicity. With the timing, you have to consider that there just might be some sort of divine intervention."

Randa points out a series of peculiarly linked events that led Emily to leap a gate at a slaughterhouse in Hopkinton on Nov. 14, hide out in nearby woods for the next month, and eventually find her way into the care of the Randas, that seem to be linked with Randa's own movements at the time.

Lately, there has been something of a mundane intervention into Emily's saga. Calls have been placed to the Randas by a movie producer, the Associated Press, and most recently, People Magazine, all seeking the particulars of the story.

No one seems immune from putting his or her own spin on the cow's tale of survival. Political satirist Barry Crimins, said Randa, stayed with the cow's keepers last week, gathering material on Emily for his show last Friday at Passim Coffee House in Cambridge.

SPECIAL TALE

All the recent attention, however, obscures the essential appropriateness of the story.

If the Randas had sat down to write a parable for the Peace Abbey – a center for the study and practice of nonviolence and cruelty-free living -- they couldn't have come up with a better tale than the one initiated by Emily seven weeks ago, when she jumped out of the Arena slaughterhouse on Nov. 14 and survived in the neighboring woods.

"Our philosophy at the Abbey," said Randa, "is one that really tries to instill a sense of compassion and the power to reach beyond one's own limitations and help others."

"We have a long history of peace education at the Abbey's school to help students learn about people who make a difference in the world. Emily is another spoke in the wheel of service and the center of that wheel is compassion, that essential element that helps make the world a less harsh and more loving place."

Strictly speaking, the saga of Emily began near Halloween, even before she jumped the gate out of the building. Randa took a group of students to the Food for the Needy Farm in Hopkinton to help the owner, Bill Abbot, pick tomatoes. On the way to the farm, said Randa, she and the students passed the Arena slaughterhouse.

"As an animal lover and an animal rights activist, I became fairly obsessed with the image of the trailer with the animals being driven to their death. I couldn't sleep that night."

Two weeks later Emily escaped, hiding out in the woods adjacent to where, two weeks earlier, Randa had been picking tomatoes. It wasn't until mid-December, however, that Randa discovered a cow from the slaughterhouse had run away into the woods.

"I definitely felt like the stage had been set beforehand," she said. "I decided I had to take action."

She and her husband Lewis struck an agreement on Dec. 19 with Frank Arena, the owner of the slaughterhouse, to buy the fugitive cow for $1.

The next day the Randas were out in the woods with a bucket of grain, trying to coax Emily out of hiding. On Thursday, after the snowstorm, she and her husband were able to track the cow to a secluded spot in the woods.

EARNING TRUST

It took nearly four more days to earn the cow's trust, said Randa. On Saturday, two friends, David and Amy Moore of Sherborn, came out to help, and Bill Greaves of Norfolk brought his livestock trailer out to the clearing in the woods. And on Sunday -- Christmas Eve -- the Randas with friends assisting them managed to get Emily, secured by a rope, into the trailer.

In the week or so since, Emily the cow has become something of a tourist attraction. People drop by daily for a chance to pet the celebrity. "She seems to be very adaptable," said Randa. "She was a little shaky at first. She was pretty traumatized. Once she realized she was in a safe haven, she was fine. She was licking our hands that evening. She appears to truly care about people and exudes a quality of affection that is palpable. She is amazing."

"She has made friends with the two horses in the barn. And she has had a constant flow of visitors.

"She seems to be basking in the limelight."

COW GETS MEATY PROFILE IN "PEOPLE MAGAZINE"

By Rodney M. Schussler

From the chopping block to doctor's waiting rooms across the nation. Emily, that lovable 2 year-old Holstein spared from the butcher's knife by a local family, has gone national. After stealing the hearts -- and appetites-- of MetroWest residents, the cow who braved the cold Hopkinton backwoods for five weeks before being rescued is featured in this week's People magazine.

The writer and photographer from the magazine visited the Peace Abbey in Sherborn on Dec. 30, sharing some bovine time with the rescued animal.

The one-page spread, titled "Profile in Cowage," features a quirky summary of Emily's saga -- her escape from the Arena slaughterhouse in Hopkinton, her survival for 40 days and 40 nights in the woods and her ultimate rescue by the Randa family.

HOLY COW
PROFILE IN COWRAGE

With a stake in not becoming a steak,
Emily survives life on the lam

Cancel the Emilyburger! Emily the cow, a 2-year-old Holstein heifer, was all set to walk her last mile on Nov. 14 at the A. Arena & Sons slaughterhouse in Hopkinton, Massachusetts, west of Boston, when she decided her future wasn't behind her. Making a prodigious -- and very unbovine -- five-foot vertical leap over a holding-pen gate, off a dock and into local legend, she fled to the woods outside town, where she hung out with a herd of deer, dined at a nearby farm, made cameo appearances in downtown Hopkinton and honed her evasion skills. Like some bovine Pimpernel, she was sought everywhere but never captured. "We had her cornered a bunch of times," says Paul Arena, 40, son of Frank Arena, owner of the slaughterhouse, "but we just couldn't get her."

As word of Emily's exploits spread, people began leaving hay for her in fields and backyards. After a story ran in the regional *Middlesex News,* animal lovers Robert Ahearn, Ernest Clark, and Meg Randa stepped in. Randa and her husband, Lewis, vegetarians who run a school for young people with special needs, decided to buy Emily -- who was named, following her escape, by Paul Arena's 4-year-old daughter Angela after her best friend -- so she could join the school's goat, two horses and pair of rabbits. Even the Arenas got into the spirit. First, they reduced the price from $500 to $350 because Emily had run off some of her value. Then, moved by the thought of the cow's helping the school, they dropped the price to $1.

Accompanied by a band of sympathizers, the save-Emily forces began their hunt. "All I could think of was Emily out there in the snow," says Randa, who finally made contact with the cow in the woods about a mile from the slaughterhouse. She and Lewis even announced to Emily that they didn't use any animal products. Finally, at 8:35a.m on Christmas Eve, lured by a bucket of grain and no small amount of pulling, Emily was coaxed into a trailer and taken to the Peace Abbey's school in nearby Sherborn. She has already been cow-of-honor at a human wedding in the barn. "I think," says Randa, "that she really knows she's a very lucky cow."

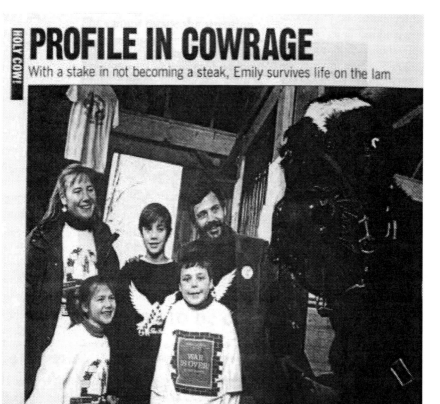

PROFILE IN COWRAGE
With a stake in not becoming a steak, Emily survives life on the lam

A "Emily (right) gives the vegetarian movement a face," says Meg Randa (with Lewis and kids Abbey, 6, Christopher, 12, and Mikey, 8).

ENOUGH WITH THE SENTIMENT, PLEASE PASS THE VEAL

By Earl Henry Sholley

I am writing this while eating a veal heart. I love the consistency and subtle gamey flavor of this tender organ. Some people eat to live. Not this epicurean. I live to eat. The dinner table is the center of my life in my very comfortable universe. I suppose that being raised by wolves like Romulus and Remus is responsible for turning me into a carnivore. Once you get that taste of blood, carotene is a pretty dull flavor.

Worse than a liberal in denial is a holier than thou veginutic. I have this recurring nightmare that Lucifer is a vegetarian, and mortal sinners cannot eat meat in the afterlife. I can't think of a better reason for staying on the straight and narrow. Do these people ever contemplate being lost in the jungle, and hoping and praying that they encounter a vegi-tiger? Being a vegi-macro whatever would not save them. That would take a rifle and a well-placed bullet. Reality check! Where do these people come from? I am convinced it has something to do with salt water and rock music.

Call me old fashioned, but I was taught that God put man in dominion over the animals so that he and she might live. After all, the Burpee seed catalog is a somewhat recent phenomenon. God help us that someone should discover that plants are people too. Personally, I love animals. They are so versatile. They make great pets, companions, food, clothing, tools and great beasts of burden. God really knew what He was doing when He gave us the animals. The Amish have no time for this nonsense. They sincerely believe that their abundance comes from the Lord. They constantly pray for a double portion of everything. Das pot roast is sehr gut.

Gabriel, Emily's companion who was rescued from his fate as a veal calf. (Photo by Lewis Randa)

Ever notice how many movie stars and musicians are into the occult, drugs, sex, suicide and vegetarianism? Why is that? They are carnivores of a different sort. Ironically, we have more eating disorders in America than probably the rest of the combined industrial world. Can anyone doubt the negative influence of the fringe elements in our society? Nirvana for them must be a sacred cow named Emily. I wonder what they feed their cats? Please pass the veal.

SNOWFALL
As measured by Kennedy School students

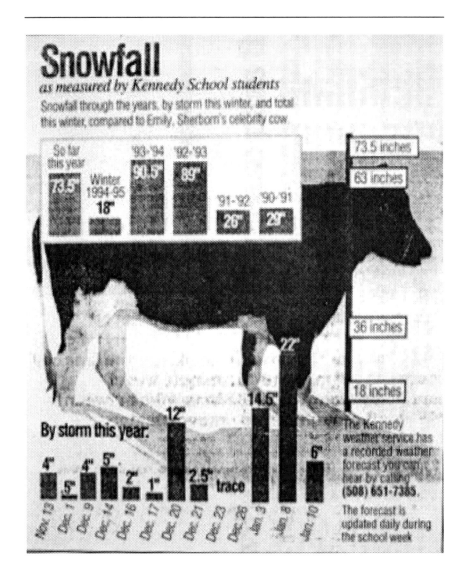

Abbey Randa plays the guitar while Emily sings along. (Photo by Meg Randa)

ANIMALS AS FRIENDS

By Evelyn B. Kimber

It was hard to tell whether the letter to the editor was serious or attempting humor in his commentary "please pass the veal" (Jan. 14). However, the implication that humans' selfish, even abusive use of animals has divine sanction is a point worth discussing.

Like the writer, many of us were "taught that God put man in dominion over animals." Parents, too, have dominion over their children. This does not give license to abuse or exploit them. Let us not interpret dominion as domination, but rather as caring stewardship.

I would not argue that animals are a gift from God, but only that they are a more delightful gift than most people may now be availing themselves of. Animals, consumed as meat, are a major contributor to heart disease, certain cancers, and a host of serious afflictions that disable and shorten life. What kind of a gift is that? Animals, as friends and fascinating co-inhabitants of our world, enhance our enjoyment of life in a healthy way.

Take a moment to envision the tender nurturing of a mother cow grooming her calf. Enjoy the mental image of deer grazing, of feisty chickens taking a dust bath, of pigs like "Babe" socializing, of rabbits frolicking in the field.

Now envision a slaughterhouse, a bloody plate, clogged and corroded arteries.

Which is the greater gift to your heart?

EMILY EXPLOITED

By LS Robbins

For over a week we have been reading about the salvation of Emily. Thanks to the perseverance of the Randas, one less bovine is going to slaughter. One less animal is being exploited... or is it?

Emily is a cow. She does not read People or go to the movies. She is a herd animal that does best among her own kind. Instead of making a spectacle of Emily, perhaps the Randas should consider what is best for her.

Emily with Gabe in their new home at the Peace Abbey. (Photo by Meg Randa)

SLAUGHTERHOUSE HAS PRIDE IN PRODUCT

Emily the cow places Hopkinton family business in the spotlight

By Carolyn Fretz

HOPKINTON   When Emily the Cow escaped from a local slaughterhouse just before the holidays, many people were as surprised to learn there was a slaughterhouse in the area as they were by Emily's rather un-bovine leap over a 5-foot gate out of the building.

In a region better known for high-tech, bio-tech, and info-tech companies, A. Arena & Sons makes a product to satisfy a far more basic human drive: hunger.

Workers at the plant and packinghouse slaughter about 500 animals each week. The company specializes in beef and veal. Workers cut, pack, and ship about 50,000 pounds a week to local, independently owned grocery stores.

The Hopkinton business is one of only four federally-inspected beef slaughterhouses in Massachusetts. The others are in Athol, West Groton, and Swansea, according to the USDA.

Emily, who was scheduled to be part of that total one week in November, instead spent 40 days on the run in and around Hopkinton. She became a folk hero in town, front-page news in MetroWest and a national celebrity after she appeared in People magazine.

Meg and Lewis Randa, who took the heifer in and added her to the menagerie at their school and farm in Sherborn, are negotiating with a book publisher and three Hollywood producers who want the rights to tell Emily's story.

Typical commercial meat chest with freshly killed hind sections.

Meanwhile, Frank Arena, who graciously surrendered the cow he had bought for $1, is just thankful Emily didn't cause a car wreck while she was loose and that all the media attention didn't bring out a slew of animal rights activists.

"Let's face it," Arena said with a good-natured shrug, "It's not a pleasant business. The less publicity I get the better it probably is for us."

Arena, 64, is the owner of the A. Arena & Sons. The "A" stands for Anthony, Arena's father who started the business on Ash Street 68 years ago. Today, most of the work at the slaughterhouse is done by the third generation, Frank's sons, Paul Arena, the plant foreman, and Joe Arena, the packing foreman.

All three men have powerful hands and arms that testify to years of hard work. As Frank Arena put it standing in the dirt yard outside the plant, "What job in a slaughterhouse isn't a tough job?"

"It used to be a lot tougher, though. We had to hoist the animals ourselves and pull the hides off by hand. Today a lot of that is done mechanically."

"Now that I think about it," Arena laughed as he looked back over his shoulder at the plant, "There's almost no work to do today!"

Beef hearts for fish

The Arenas buy calves, cows, and bulls at cattle auctions in Massachusetts and Connecticut. The animals come from farms all over New England.

The family also slaughters pigs, usually one day a week, and occasionally goats.

The Arenas are best known, though, for their fresh veal and calves livers which they truck to customers in Massachusetts and Rhode Island.

"Fresh meat is like fresh anything else," Arena says. "There's no comparison between a fresh calves liver and one that is a week old or one that has been frozen."

A typical calf costs Arena about $45 and yields about 50 pounds of meat that sells for about $50.

Hides sold to the manufacturers of leather products, parts and organs that go to research laboratories and leftovers shipped to a rendering plant yield another $15 per calf.

John LaRusso is a regular at the Arena plant. His company, Research 87 in Marlborough, specializes in supplying medical and veterinary laboratories with parts, such as eyes and knees.

Grocery store meat chest.

"This is the closest place to Boston," LaRusso said. "That makes it the best place for me to buy because it's important to researchers too, that everything be as fresh as possible."

Lloyd La Pan, a butcher for Roche Brothers, stopped by Arena's plant last week to pick up a couple of beef hearts.

"They're for a friend who raises tropical fish," La Pan said. "He freezes them and shaves off a little a time and mixes it in with a bunch of other stuff for the fish. I couldn't believe it when he first asked me about it. 'Beef hearts? For fish?' I said."

Regulations tough

That's the kind of order Arena's grandfather, who was a butcher in Sicily, probably never had to fill.

"A farmer would usually bring him one animal to kill," Arena said. "The farmer would pay him by letting him keep part of the animal."

"He'd make sausage from some of the meat and hang it to dry in the attic. Then, once a year he'd take all the sausage he'd made into town and trade it for flour and sugar and whatever else he needed."

Arena's father, Anthony Arena, came to the United States in 1914, and worked in a piano factory, opened a barber shop and eventually moved to Hopkinton to start a dairy farm and slaughterhouse in 1928. The dairy operation stopped in 1957.

Anthony Arena died in 1968, and his son took over the business.

At its peak the company employed 15 full-time workers. That's down to seven now, even though the profit margin in the business has grown from 2 percent a generation ago to 6 to 8 percent today, Arena said.

Expenses are up too, he said, with insurance running $45,000 and electricity $4,000 a month.

But those fluctuations in cost and profits pale next to the changes in local and world markets that are bringing new and potentially overwhelming, economic pressure to bear on small-time operators likes the Arenas.

* Consumption of red meat is down in the U.S, said Anne McGuigan, spokeswoman for the U.S Dept. of Agriculture.

* New trade agreements make it easier for other countries to export beef to the U.S, driving prices here down.

* There are a lot of cattle around now, "Arena said, "It happens every few years, but this time it's worse because of the imports. There's everything from live cattle to processed meat coming in from Mexico, Canada -- all over."

* Consolidation, a trend in many industries, is occurring in the grocery and supermarket business, too.

Stop & shop and the other big stores are putting all the mom and pops out of business," Arena said. "The big stores want 40,000 pounds of meat at a time. I can't give them that, and I'm running out of people I can do business with."

* New USDA regulations created to stop the spread of deadly strains of E. coli bacteria may be too expensive for small slaughterhouses to implement.

Slaughterhouses may be required to have in-house laboratories to test for the presence of some contaminants, McGuigan said. Big operations, like a nearby plant in Manchester, N.H, that procures 80,000 pounds of hamburger an hour and others out west that slaughter as many as 300 animals an hour, will be able to absorb the cost, but Arena isn't sure he can.

"That's what I like least about the business," Paul Arena said. "The federal regulations. It's funny because they're making people like us a dying breed, and that's what I like best about the business -- trying to keep it going."

Escape clause

Frank Arena plans to leave that fight to his sons. He's ready to retire. He says he won't miss his office cluttered with receipts, more than a few Christmas boxes of Seagram's VO, a shotgun and an American flag. And he won't miss haggling with buyers and sellers alike.

Frank Arena sees himself in the near future sitting on a front porch -- maybe at a dairy farm in Vermont or somewhere in East Tennessee, where his best friend lives.

All the hard work will fade away as he tells his tales of Emily the cow and the bull that escaped years before only to be shot by Framingham police in full view of a restaurant full of diners at the now defunct Red Coach Grill.""That was one shot I was glad I missed," said Arena, who was also in pursuit of the bull.

IS VEGETARIANISM OUR DESTINY?

By Beverly G. Rich

L.S Robbins, V.M.D, recently wrote an opinion piece ("Emily Exploited?" Jan. 14) suggesting that Meg and Lewis Randa may be exploiting Emily, the cow they rescued after she jumped a five-foot gate to escape the slaughterhouse.

As a volunteer at the Peace Abbey and Greater Boston Vegetarian Resource Center, I have seen the Randas at work. They act not for personal gain, but in support of their principles and in pursuit of their visions.

Dr. Robbins, on the other hand, failed to divulge her own bias in this matter. As a veterinarian for dairy cattle such as Emily, who are ultimately sent to slaughter, she works with the industry from which Emily fled.

Is it exploitation to share Emily's inspirational story with the world? Or is the exploitation the way we treat animals -- as a commodity to be used and abused at our will and whim? For one answer, look to another Robbins -- John Robbins, who turned his back on the Baskin-Robbins ice cream empire his father would have passed on to him. Instead, he has worked to counter the devastation perpetuated by the meat and dairy industries.

What might Emily's life had been like, "among her own kind?" According to John Robbins, author of "Diet for a new America," most dairy cows in this country do not lead an idyllic life. Many are chained at the neck and lined up in cramped, narrow stalls, as in a factory assembly line, and fed and milked by machines where they stand. Others are confined 24 hours a day for 10 months of the year to a tiny "Unicar," a kind of cage on wheels which is rolled to the milking apparatus, and in which they are 'unable to walk or turn around.' In most cases Dairy cattle have little or no opportunity to act as a herd, and almost no chance to employ their natural maternal instincts.

A cow normally gives milk for one reason: she just had a calf. In order to keep the milk flowing, it's necessary to keep impregnating the cow; that's what a dairy farmer does. Every year he calls a breeder who comes along and artificially (and forcefully) inseminates his cows.

Cows carry calves for nine months and, after a grueling labor session, give birth to 80 - to 100 - pound offspring. Normally cows lactate to nourish their calf. But the farmer lets a calf suckle for a few days, then takes it away from its mother.

It's possible to milk a cow for about 6 to 8 months before she dries up. So what do they do? Artificially inseminate her again. Finally, after a few years of producing calves and milk, a cow's production drops and she's shipped off to the slaughterhouse.

What happens to the calves which are the byproducts of dairy production? A female calf goes on to repeat her mother's fate: a male calf faces a brief, inhumane life as a veal calf. Male dairy calves, writes Robbins, are confined to tiny, darkened stalls in which they can barely move. They are fed a formula intended to make them anemic and fat as well as high doses of antibiotics and other drugs (some toxic to humans) to replace the immunity provided by the mother's milk. Some calves may go blind. At four months, they are shipped to the slaughterhouse. This process yields the maximum amount of pale and tender veal meat from each calf.

Even those who believe we have a right to make use of animals for food and other products cannot deny their pain and suffering. Why do we use animals this way? Many of us grew up believing that animal products were necessary for our health. However, we have learned that, not only are they unnecessary, but can be detrimental to our health. After years of delay, the U.S Department of Agriculture has finally acknowledged that a vegetarian diet can be nutritionally complete.

Why not stop the abuse and exploitation of farm animals? We could feed more people. According to Robbins, the same amount of farm land needed to raise cattle could feed more than six times as many vegetarians than meat-eaters. We could reduce heart disease and other illnesses which are aggravated by a high-fat diet. We could save vast quantities of water now being diverted to support of animal agriculture.

Thoreau once wrote: "I have no doubt that it is part of the destiny of the human race in its gradual development to leave off the eating of animals." I truly hope he was right.

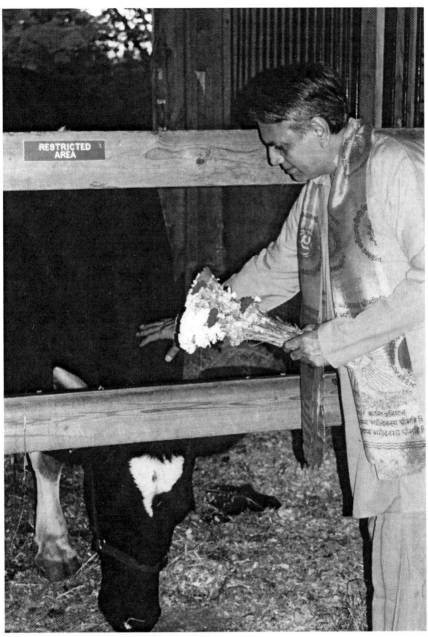

*Emily receives flowers from Hindu Disciple / Priest
Nityanand Patel. (Photo by Lewis Randa)*

A MIRACLE SAVED EMILY

By Nityanand Patel

On November 14, 1995 a cow named Emily escaped the Arena slaughterhouse in Holliston, MA, leaping over the five-foot high gate out of the building. It roamed in and out of the woods and struggled to find food in a bitterly cold winter. People spotted her in the woods, in back yards, feeding with other animals like deer. The owner of the slaughterhouse desperately tried to catch her but failed to do so.

One family tried to rescue her. Their valiant efforts were also not immediately fruitful, but they did not give up hope. Then a miracle happened. The cow became cooperative enough to get into a trailer provided by the Randa family and received a new home.

Emily's original owner showed kindness by selling her for $1 to the family. The media showed great interest in the whole episode. A Hollywood agency came forward seeking to turn the story into a movie. People Magazine editors wrote a feature on Emily. Some even thought it would make an exciting story for a children's book.

How was it that the fugitive cow was rescued on Christmas Eve? Was there an unseen power behind this? Was she a gift from God?

Despite the coverage, many non-vegetarians still did not rethink their red meat diet. Are they doing wrong?

Let us attack some fundamental issues. Are humans basically vegetarian or non-vegetarian? A comparison between animals helps us decide. Consider the structure of teeth in vegetarian and non-vegetarian animals. Blunt, grinding teeth and molar teeth are found in vegetarian animals as compared to sharp, bite-to-tear teeth found in non-vegetarian animals. Look at the nails or claws of vegetarian and non-vegetarian animals. Vegetarians have short, blunt nails while non-vegetarian animals have long, sharp claws. Consider the presence of sweat glands on the tongue of non-vegetarian animals and compare that with the tongue of a horse or a cow. The length of the intestine also determines the type of food creatures are meant to consume. Compare a length of 33 feet for humans to just 12 feet for a lion. What conclusion do these comparisons bring? We are basically vegetarian animals.

I would like to urge readers to examine their food choices in light of Emily's story. Is it not a miracle that Emily freed herself on Nov. 14, the day when world-renowned worshipper of Peace, India's Prime Minster Jawaharlal Nehru was born? Emily succeeded in finding shelter in one of the few places outside India where you will find a statue of the worshipper of the cow and vegetarian father of India, Mahatma Gandhi. And all of this occurred on Christmas Eve.

THAT DARN COW AGAIN

By David Traub

SHERBORN   MetroWest's cow celebre had a bash to celebrate over a month of freedom yesterday in what would be her last photo op before filming for a movie starts.

Yes, it looks like the tale of the cow that spent 40 days wandering the wilderness of Hopkinton after leaping a slaughterhouse fence could land on the big screen.

But Lewis Randa, whose family adopted Emily, said he isn't going to let Hollywood make hamburger out of a story he considers as important as it has been entertaining.

"There will be a motion picture," Randa said, adding that a producer who worked on the recent film of an updated version of Shakespeare's "Richard III" has been in contact with his family about the cow's tale.

"It is not going to be some trivialized thing about a cow showing people how to be brave," he said. "Ahh, no thank you. That was "Free Willy," he said, referring to a movie about a killer whale's journey to freedom.

Lewis and Meg Randa operate the Greater Boston Vegetarian Resource Center, the Peace Abbey, and the Life Experience School for special needs children. The couple and two of their three children are vegetarians. Meg and Lewis also eschew dairy products and any goods made from animals skins or wools.

The movie, Lewis Randa said, will use the story of Emily's flight from the slaughterhouse to show what happens to animals on the way to the supermarket.

Yesterday's party was a chance for the Randas to thank the two or three dozen people who helped get Emily from the woods to the barn behind the Abbey.

Emily scratching her neck on the straps of her stall at the Abbey. (Photo by Stephen Tackeff, Middlesex News)

Bob Ahearn, who first spotted the bovine in the woods behind his Hopkinton home, was there. David and Amy Moore, friends who care for cows in Sherborn and Bill Greaves, who supplied the livestock trailer used to bring Emily to Sherborn, were there. Newlyweds Heather Ralph Tamashian and Gary Tamashian, young vegetarians who exchanged rings in Emily's presence Dec. 29, where there visiting their biggest bridesmaid -- who Meg Randa said has put on about 100 pounds since leaving the snowy woods for a warm barn and a steady diet of oats.

So in a society where anniversary gifts are traditionally worn, Emily got three dozen visitors and a fistful of carrots.

Maybe there was nothing at Marshall's that fit.

THE REAL-LIFE EMILY

By Wesley Britton

The epic of Emily the Cow began in November 1995 when a then-unnamed two-year-old Holstein, scheduled for the slaughterhouse, decided "Oh-h-h-no-o-o you don't". She leaped over the five-foot killing floor gate and disappeared into the local woods near Hopkinton, Massachusetts, west of Boston. "For forty days & forty nights," Emily hung out with a herd of deer, made occasional appearances at a nearby farm in downtown Hopkinton, and became a *cause celebre* in regional newspapers.

Local folks began leaving hay for her in fields and backyards even as the butchers failed time after time to capture the Holstein Houdini. Then, teachers at a school for youth with special needs decided to buy Emily and allow her to live out her life with the school's goat, two horses and pair of rabbits. At first, the butchers wanted $350 (discounted for her lost weight) but ultimately sold a town legend for $1 to the vegetarians at the Peace Abbey.

At 8:35 A.M on Christmas Eve, 1995, after pointing out to Emily that they were vegetarians and didn't even use animal parts, the leaders of the Peace Abbey lured Emily to her own special barn in nearby Sherborn. At the Abbey, Emily now is honored with her own shrine, her walls covered with newspaper accounts of her exploits in the *Boston Globe*, People magazine and appropriately, a copy of this poem. She has even been cow-of-honor at a human wedding held in her barn and a subject of a traveling humorist's one-man show. With the publication of "Emily the cow" in two languages here at the *Cafe Bellas Artes,* Emily's story is now part of world literature, with a life that will go well beyond her justly honored earthly existence.

La vaca Emily
(Emily the cow)

Traduccion por Antonio Salazar

Segura de su destino,
Ella brinco le cerca de establo
y viendo por la velocidad de su andar,
ella claramenta no estaba en humor para aceptar la predestinacion.

Por cuerenta dias y cuarenta noches,
Ella vivo con las venados en el bosque
pero cuando la encontraron fue corta la lucha para
recapturar a lot pequeno vaca que pudo.

Doscientas libras perido de su cincha,
ya inservible para la matanza del carcinero.
Ellos determinaron que un dolar era todo lo que valia
entonces el Templo de la Paz la compro
para que pudiera paster en sus jardines
rodiada por vegetarianos.

Emily the cow (a true story)
Wesley Britton

Knowing her fate,
She cleared the stable fence
& at the rate of her gait
was clearly in no mood for predestination.

For forty days & forty nights
She lived with the deer in the woods
but when they found her it took little fight
to recapture the little cow that could.

Two hundred pounds were lost from her girth,
now unfit for the butcher's kill.
They determined one dollar was all she was worth
so the Peace Temple bought her
to graze on their grounds
surrounded by vegetarians.

A COW WHO TOOK MATTERS
INTO HER OWN HOOVES

Emily the cow found herself on the killing floor of the slaughterhouse in Hopkinton, Massachusetts in November 1995, when she evidently decided she would rather be free. The two-year-old, 1,800 pound Holstein heifer bravely leaped over a five-foot gate out of the building. For 40 days and 40 nights following her daring escape, she managed to live in the woods around the town, foraging for food and hobnobbing with a herd of deer.

As the escaped cow cleverly evaded capture, people began rooting for her. Emily's partisans set out hay for her and shielded her whereabouts from authorities and from the slaughterhouses' employees. "Like some bovine pimpernel," reported People magazine, "She was sought everywhere but never captured."

Emily's story excited the interest of animal lovers Meg and Lewis Randa, who have given many animals sanctuary at the Life Experience School, a school for children with special needs in Sherborn, Massachusetts. The A. Arena & Sons slaughterhouse ended up selling Emily to the Randas for $1, reasoning that the cow had run off much of her value.

Meg Randa, who took great care to assure Emily that she and her family were vegetarians, coaxed the elusive heifer into a trailer with a bucket of feed and the helping hands of family and friends. The Randas had their Christmas dinner outside in the barn with Emily, who now lives, and serves as a teacher, at the Peace Abbey's Life Experience School.

This cow-rageous Holstein has become quite famous, as her story has appeared in countless newspaper and magazine articles around the county, as well as coverage by CBS and a forthcoming children's book.

There are rumors of a film being planned, but Emily is keeping quiet about whether she is destined to become a ruminant movie star.

Emily has become something of a cult figure, as sympathizers have pledged in her presence to stop eating meat. She has also been bovine-of-honor at a human wedding that took place in the Abbey's barn.

DON'T HAVE A COW, EMILY'S BACK

Sherborn bovine is spokescow for Great American Meatout

By Bonne Docherty

Lewis and Meg Randa will be flipping burgers in Sherborn today to celebrate the Great American Meat out.

Veggie burgers, that is.

Meg said she plans to offer at least four varieties although she (and Chelsea Clinton) prefers Boca Burgers.

And if the weather is warm, guests will join Emily, slaughterhouse escapee and the Meatout's Poster Cow, in the barn.

"The Meatout encourages people to try alternatives to eating animals like Emily," Meg Randa said. **The Great American Smoke Out** helped her brother quit smoking, and she hopes today's event will give meat-eaters a similar opportunity, she said.

Meg said she and her husband went vegan, giving up all animal products, at the MIT Meatout three years ago.

The Great American Meatout encourages people to give up meat for at least one day. It started in 1985 with 35 events and now has over 1,000 events across the country, according to National Director Scott Williams.

Local events include the Randas' cookout at noon at the Peace Abbey in Sherborn, and a 7 P.M benefit concert at Boston University. For the record, Boca Burgers, which will be served at the Randas, are made of soy, potato starch, dehydrated onions, vegetarian flavorings and spices, carrageenan and fresh garlic.

Nutritional, ethical, and environmental concerns lead many people to give up meat.

"The most common reason (to give up meat), is health," Williams said. "You can get more energy, drop pounds, and spend less money on food."

Although many consider eating meat a part of a well-balanced diet, it can increase the chances of heart attacks, cancer, and strokes.

According to Boston Vegetarian Society director Evelyn Kimber, a good diet consists of grains, fruits, vegetables, and legumes, such as lentils and beans.

Some people prefer the taste of vegetarian cooking, and international menus offer a variety of tasty non-meat options. "The fewer animal products you eat, the greater the health benefits," she said.

Others forsake hamburgers because of compassion for animals. In the United States, seven billion animals, not including fish and seafood, are killed for food every year, Kimber said.

"Many people are unaware of the holocaust of animals that occurs in slaughterhouses and the birth-to-death suffering in today's factory farms," Kimber said. "Animals are confined so there are huge numbers of animals in a small space."

"Learning about such conditions makes even people who don't love animals think twice about eating meat," she said.

Vegetarians also have a smaller environmental impact than meat eaters, Williams said. "Fewer crops (to feed animals), less pasture land and less fossil fuel means less of an environmental impact."

"And the grain used to raise meat, an inefficient way to get protein, could better be used to feed the world's hungry," Kimber said.

Emily, who leapt over a five-foot gate out of Hopkinton's Arena slaughterhouse in fall 1995, is the poster cow for this year's Meatout.

The 3-year-old Holstein gained international recognition after her escape and the poster shows her in front of several Middlesex News articles telling her story.

"Emily asks you to kick the habit," it reads. A bubble with a crossed-out steak shows Emily's sentiments.

"What could be a more compelling poster than Emily, given her story," Williams said.

Sold to and captured by the Randas, Emily now lives in a barn that doubles as the Greater Boston Vegetarian Resource Center.

Day 26 on a life raft somewhere in the North Atlantic …
Emily the Cow

EMILY, COW IN-RESIDENCE AT THE PEACE ABBEY

By Ben Tousley

It was one week before Christmas when I called Lewis Randa to see about spending New Years Eve at the Peace Abbey in Sherborn.

"What's goin' on out there?" I asked

"Well, right now," he said, "we've got our attention focused on a cow we're trying to rescue."

This statement did not greatly surprise me, for Lewis and Meg at the Peace Abbey are always lifting up and giving form to visions most of the world but dimly imagine, from the Pacifist Memorial to the Life Experience School for children with disabilities to the Registry for Conscientious Objectors and, in the past year, the Greater Boston Vegetarian Resource Center.

Lewis explained this was no ordinary cow. This was Emily the Cow, who, at two years old, was being led into the Arena slaughterhouse in Hopkinton, MA when suddenly, mysteriously, she broke free, scaled a five-foot gate out of the building (her weight at the time was over 1400 pounds) and ran off into the nearby woods where she successfully eluded hunters for 40 days and 40 nights.

At the time Meg Randa read Emily's plight in the Middlesex News, it was Dec. 19 with plenty of snow on the ground and more on the way. She was determined to do something to save Emily's life; and husband Lewis, no stranger to bold ventures, joined in helping to organize a Save Emily effort. Both had become vegetarians two years before and were becoming increasingly concerned with animal rights and the cruel treatment of animals by the dairy industry. Lewis reflects:

"Veganism is the most compassionate form of pacifism for it takes into account the blessedness of all God's creatures to who share this small planet. For decades, we in the peace movement 'marched' to end violence at home and abroad, yet many continue consuming the flesh of animals without giving a second thought to the suffering and death connected to our food choices. Gandhi, one of the greatest architects of nonviolence, taught us that true peacefulness begins with what we eat."

On December 21, Meg and Lewis contacted the Arena people to offer to buy Emily, who, with her wilderness ordeal, had lost over 500 pounds. Meanwhile, the Middlesex News began running front-page stories about Emily the week before Christmas. The story was picked up by the Associated Press and was broadcast nationally on CBS and other programs.

The following day, Arena agreed to sell Emily to the Randas for one dollar. The only problem was they didn't know exactly where to find her. So, Meg and Lewis, with two of their three children -- Michael and Abbey - began combing the woods around Hopkinton.

A few days before Christmas the Randas found Emily, and Meg, an old hand with horses, was able to lead her into a clearing with a feed bucket. Over the next several days, Meg refused the offers of more aggressive cowhands to bring Emily in and spent time befriending her. On December 23, a trailer was brought near the clearing and on Christmas Eve, with a little coaxing and pulling, Emily was brought home to the Peace Abbey's barn. The next day, the Randas joined Emily for a (vegetarian) Christmas dinner in the barn.

The story of Emily has gained national attention, with plans afoot for a children's book and, possibly, a movie. In her new home, Emily will serve as a teacher at the Life Experience School and a constant reminder of the relatedness of all creatures.

"Emily the Cow is here to remind us of the cruelty of using animals for food when a plant-based diet is healthier for ourselves, our nation, the developing world and the planet as a whole," Lewis says. "To look Emily in the eye is to come face to face with the connection between the veal calf industry and the glass of milk or slice of cheese or dish of ice cream that seem deliciously guilt-free. Emily is with us to serve as a teacher."

COURAGE AND COW-ARDICE

Pacifist, animal rights advocate
addresses students

By Catherine Walsh

HOLLISTON   A self-described liberal and pacifist who writes a nationally syndicated column for The Washington Post used big bucks and some disgusting fat to challenge several hundred teenagers' views on peace and animal rights during a high school assembly yesterday.

Coleman McCarthy, here locally to speak at Holy Cross, receive an award from the Peace Abbey in Sherborn and commune with Emily the celebrity cow, alternately riled the Holliston students and drew their applause.

"The next time you go to Wendy's ask for a corpse-burger, - medium rare," McCarthy said, telling students that hamburgers are part of the 'war on animals'.

Students were unconvinced -- and said so loudly. "It's survival of the fittest," shouted one. Another said she was a "born-again meat eater," and argued that animals also eat animals.

"Ask yourself a simple question," McCarthy responded, "Did it have a mother? If so, don't eat it."

Students cheered when he asked them if they wanted a hamburger and fries, until he reached into a bag and pulled out a glass cylinder containing six inches of waxy-white lard.

"This is the amount of animal fat that goes into a burger, fries and shake," he said handing the fat to members of the crowd who groaned with disgust.

"If the ethical argument against killing animals for food doesn't convince you, maybe the health argument will," he said.

Emily looks over fence to greet Washington Post columnist Coleman McCarthy.
(Photo by Ed Hopfmann, Middlesex News)

McCarthy also took a $100 bill out of his wallet, placed it on the speaker's lectern and said he would give it to any student who could identify six people he called "peace breakers" and peacemakers.

Paul Revere? Robert E. Lee? Ulysses S. Grant?

All of the students raised their hands.

Harold Hughes? Jennette Rankin? Dorothy Day?

Silence fell over the high school auditorium. One student identified Dorothy Day as the founder of the Catholic Worker movement, an anarchist and a pacifist who fed and housed the poor.

Harold Hughes, a senator from Iowa, was the only man in U.S History to leave congress, saying he was sickened by weapons proliferations, McCarthy said.

Jennette Rankin, the first woman member of congress, voted against the first and second World Wars and lost elections for her House of Representatives seat following each vote.

"She said you could no more win a war than win an earthquake," McCarthy said, adding "You know all about the peace-breakers, but not the peacemakers."

McCarthy also urged the teens to reject violence, but only a handful said they would be interested in a peace studies program at the school.

Later, at a meeting with the school newspaper staff, he urged members of the senior class to give a class gift of 'peace volumes' by authors such as Martin Luther King Jr. and Mahatma Gandhi to the high school library.

Back at the Peace Abbey, where he received a 'courage of conscience award' earlier in the day, McCarthy flirted with Emily, the cow who escaped from a Hopkinton slaughterhouse, and hid in the woods for six weeks before being taken in as a symbol of vegetarianism by the Randa family that runs the Peace Abbey.

"You're gorgeous, gorgeous," he murmured, stroking Emily's forehead.

'MAD COW' RESPONSE MAKES THE COW MAD

By Emily the Cow, Guest Bovine Columnist

Imagine this, I'm relaxing in my stall at the Peace Abbey where I live in exile, having recently escaped from a slaughterhouse, when I overhear someone in the barn say "so they might have to slaughter the nation's herd." To my hooves I jump, posthaste. "Excuse me," I moo, "Slaughter the nation's herd? Have they no shame?"

Then I flash on my worst nightmare: Oh no, it's come true! they've gone and honored Ronald McDonald with a national holiday. And you know what that means for us cows. It won't be a pretty sight. Then I remember the number of cows killed, or was it hamburgers served on the Golden Arches. Guess Ronald McDonald has a different Golden Rule.

Then the fella goes on to say, "Great Britain has an outbreak of -- get this -- mad cow disease" with people dying all over the place from eating meat. What's wrong with this picture? "Mad cow disease." -- I don't think so. Sounds more like mad human disease to this cud chewin' heifer. Eating a corpse, any corpse for that matter, is always risky business. Sooner of later using your stomach as a graveyard is bound to do you in. Even with four stomachs, I know better than to try that!

Now don't get me wrong, I feel sorry for those who died from eating cows, just as I feel sorry for tens of millions of fellow cows, pigs, chickens and turkeys killed every day as food for people.

Anyway, I've got this great idea -- instead of slaughtering all the cows in England for fear of getting mad cow disease, why not load up all the cows on big barges and send them off to the Falkland Islands, which Britain went to war over with Argentina a while back, and put them out to graze to live out their lives in peace? Then the British could become vegetarians like us cows and everyone would be better off and healthier, too.

And you know it saddens me to think that as "Babe", a British-style film about a pig came up for several Oscars, families in the UK mourning the deaths of their loved ones who died from eating meat won't make the connection between their story and Babe's.

And to think they call it "mad cow disease".

Now really.

WHAT HAPPENED TO NO MEAT ON FRIDAYS?

By Emily the Cow, Guest Bovine Columnist

Following several threatening phone calls into the Abbey office regarding my column (guess certain meat eaters don't have much of an appetite for bovine satire) Lewis, my personal attendant, thought it best that I lay low so I retired as a contributing columnist and wondered what could have been. ?!?

Living in sanctuary at the Peace Abbey as a fugitive from the grocer's meat chest has many benefits beyond being kept a safe distance from the slaughterhouse. For one thing, I get to meet extraordinary people from all over the world.

Not long ago, Rosemary Von Trapp of Sound of Music fame stopped by the barn to say hello, as did Chicago Seven peace activist Dave Dellinger and his wife Elizabeth. Historian Howard Zinn stopped by, too. Each knows what being on the run is all about. At some point in their lives, each had to high tail it out of town like I had to, not all that long ago.

Recently, Father Daniel Berrigan, former fugitive and anti-war priest, stopped by the barn to say hello. After he left I could have kicked myself for not asking the question every cow has been wondering about ever since Vatican II: "Why did the Catholic Church stop making eating meat on Friday a sin?"

To think, people used to have to confess eating us cows as a sin and ask for forgiveness. Granted, it was only on Fridays, but it was a start.

The reasons for meat abstinence on Fridays must have been numerous. Topping the list was probably reverence for life, compassion for all living creatures, self discipline, purity and holiness. From this cow's point of view, these attributes seem sorely lacking in the human family these days.

Factory farming of veal calves, pigs, chickens and turkeys suggest a lack of conscience on the part of present day civilization. Swearing off meat one day a week would at least allow folks to take stock in what they're putting in their mouths the other six days. If parochial schools, and all schools for that matter, took field trips to the nearest slaughterhouse, then abstaining from meat on Fridays might make a much needed comeback.

According to John Robbins, author of the book "Diet for a New America," the 60,000 people who die of starvation each day throughout the world could be fed if Americans reduced their meat consumption by just 10 percent.

How so you ask? By using the land to grow food for people instead of us cows -- that's how! More than 75 percent of everything grown in America is consumed by cattle. An acre of land can yield 250 pounds of hamburger meat, compared to more than 35,000 pounds of cholesterol free, high protein potatoes, corn, wheat and soy.

So let's bring back those meatless Fridays, only this time I should hope it reflects Albert Schweitzer's humanitarianism, John Robbin's ecological awareness, and St. Francis' compassion for animals. When I see Father Daniel Berrigan again, I'll be sure to bring up the subject as food for thought. *Bon appetit!*

Abbey Randa proudly shows Emily the ribbons she won in an equestrian competition. Emily reaches through the railing to see if she can get a taste of them! (Photo by Meg Randa)

ANIMALS AND YOUNG PEOPLE
Did this cow jump over the moon?
No, Emily just jumped over the fence.
But she landed in cow heaven!

By Fina Bruce

Emily the cow flew over the fence and fled into the woods near Sherborn, Massachusetts, to escape the slaughterhouse. For the next six weeks she hid from police, slaughterhouse workers and animal control officers. She lived mostly off the land but also stole from the back porches of kind people whose hearts she'd also stolen.

Two of Emily's well-wishers, Lewis and Meg Randa, decided to rescue Emily and give her a new home at the Peace Abbey's Life Experience School. They offered the slaughterhouse $500 (but only paid $1.00) to let them catch the cow and the slaughterhouse owner agreed.

With help from a group of well-wishers the Randas eventually managed to get a rope looped around Emily's neck and load her into a trailer for her journey to a new life.

Now, Emily the cow's gentle loving eyes shine with contentment, as youthful hands lovingly groom her in the barn behind the Abbey. Emily was an immediate hit with the students, who care for the school's two horses, two bunnies, one goat -- and now, one cow.

The doctrines of pacifism, the peace movement, and St. Francis of Assisi -- known for his love of animals -- shape the Abbey programs. Meanwhile, Emily's life has become humane, meaningful, and these days, famous. A movie producer has contacted the Randas expressing interest in Emily's story.

But for now, Emily seems content in her even more important role -- as gentle friend and teacher to a group of special young people.

SHERBORN FAMILY HONORS EMILY'S RESCUERS

By Allison Connolly

SHERBORN   As Emily the Cow contentedly chewed grass yesterday in a field behind the Peace Abbey, her caretakers dedicated her new barn and honored the people who helped save her and other animals destined for slaughter.

Emily captured national attention last November when she jumped a 5-foot metal gate at the Arena Slaughterhouse in Hopkinton, just minutes before she was to be killed.

On the run for more than five weeks, she was found and quickly adopted by the Randas. Since then, Emily's story has been heralded by animal rights activists and vegetarians who object to the slaughter of animals for consumption.

"We can't save every cow," said Meg Randa, who with husband Lewis adopted the 3 year-old cow shortly after she was found. "But indeed, Emily is truly an ambassador."

The Randas, who operate the Peace Abbey and Life Experience School for special needs students, yesterday honored two couples and held a fundraising potluck dinner and walk-a-thon for one of them.

Bill and Rose Abbot were honored for their work growing fresh produce on their Elmwood Farm in Hopkinton for area soup kitchens and people in need; Gene and Lori Bauston were honored for their two farms, where they keep animals they rescue from slaughterhouses and stockyards across the country.

Each couple received a white marble statue of a white dove taking flight from the palms of two opens hands. Past recipients of the Courage and Consciousness Award include Mother Teresa, Muhammad Ali, and poet Maya Angelou.

At the party celebrating Emily, Sue Schlotterbeck with daughters Jamie (7) and Sarah (9) from Holliston bring flowers and have chat with Meg Randa. (Photo by Stephen Tackeff, Middlesex News)

"There was no attention being focused on the plight of farm animals," said Gene Bauston about why he started the Farm Sanctuary 10 years ago. "They're seen as a commodity, as hunks of meat. We want people to get to know the animals as feeling beings. Then naturally, we won't eat them."

Ironically, the Abbot's farm served as Emily's hideout for the five weeks she was missing.

"It was a wonderful connection, "Meg Randa said." "No one was as needy as Emily at the time."

Emily was honored with the dedication of a new wooden barn behind the Abbey, which she will share with her horse friends, Shoshone and Jessica.

The Abbey's vegetarian potluck supper and a bike and walk-a-thon yesterday raised money for the Bauston's farms in upstate New York on a recent trip.

118

Almost 50 people carried signs urging passersby to "Go Vegetarian" on their 4-mile trek through Sherborn's Natural Preserve. Lewis Randa led 10 bikers from the Hopkinton Slaughterhouse where Emily escaped certain death to her sanctuary at the Abbey as a tribute to her.

Bolston resident Joanne Klauer, who participated in yesterday's hike, said she adopted four turkeys from the Bauston's New York farm on a recent trip.

"They're so companionable and loving," she said of her new pets. "They're so easy to take care of."

Klauer, wearing a "Please don't eat the animals" sweatshirt, said becoming a vegetarian six years ago was the best decision she'd ever made.

Boston Vegetarian Society member John Calabria of Maynard went vegetarian almost a year ago.

"It's sad what we do in the name of food," he said. "I had a hard time differentiating between my pets and what we call food, so I gave it up. Now I feel better mentally and physically."

ESCAPEE COW'S STORY TO BE TOLD IN A MAJOR MOTION PICTURE

By Bob Tremblay and Carol Beggy

SHERBORN   Lights, camera, cow.

Emily goes to Hollywood. Actually, it's her story that's going there. In fact, in July, Hollywood came to Emily to set into motion the motion picture about the rebellious bovine now residing comfortably in a barn at the Peace Abbey in Sherborn.

That Emily the cow should come to the attention of the folks in the movie business should come as no surprise to anyone familiar with the story. Scheduled for a one-way trip to the slaughterhouse in Hopkinton nearly a year ago, the plucky Emily hurdled over a five-foot-high gate -- no small task for a 1,400 pound critter -- and escaped to the freedom of the town's woods.

Her 5 1/2 weeks on the lam were duly documented by the Middlesex News and the Emily saga had begun. Aware of her plight, residents in the area left food outside for her. Still, the harsh winter weather took its toll on Emily, who dropped about 500 pounds during her exodus.

Enter the Randas. "We heard about Emily in the Middlesex News," says Meg Randa, who runs the Peace Abbey and the Life Experience School with her husband Lewis. "Someone was quoted as saying 'If I had a place, I'd keep her myself.' I then said to myself, 'We do.' It was a gut reaction."

Helping spur the Randas on was their recent commitment to vegetarianism. "We felt an emotional and moral feeling to do something to help her," Meg Randa says. It only seemed appropriate the couple's dedications to compassion and pacifism for humans should be extended to animals.

120

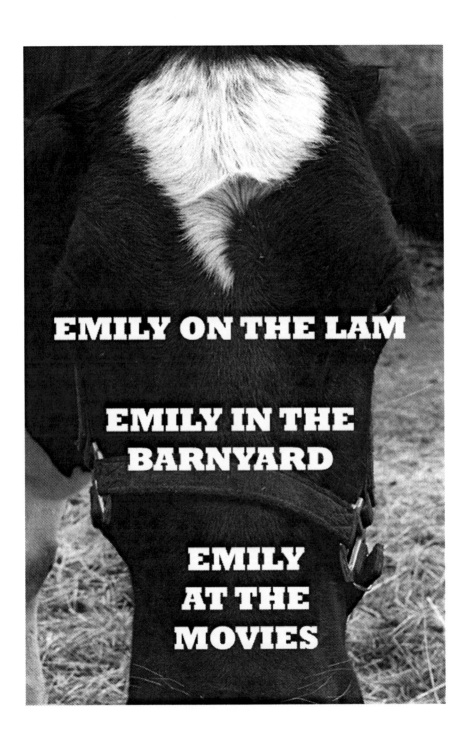

EMILY ON THE LAM

EMILY IN THE
BARNYARD

EMILY
AT THE
MOVIES

Ellen Little with husband Rob arrive from Los Angeles to meet Emily the Cow and assume a leadership role in making her story a major motion picture. (Photo by Ken McGagh, Middlesex News)

The Randas then called Frank Arena, who owned the slaughterhouse, and told him of their desire to provide sanctuary for Emily. "He originally wanted $500, then $350, and then he said he'd sell her to us for $1," says Randa.

Then the Randas had to find the wayward cow. "It took us 24 hours to track her down and about three days to earn her trust so she'd go in the trailer. We fed her grain and gave her water." The TLC approach worked.

The Randas, who already had animals in their barn, made room for Emily. "Our food budget has doubled since she's been here, but hundreds of people have come by to see her -- well-wishers visit on a daily basis -- and some leave donations that we use for her feed fund." Emily, who has since regained her weight, puts away about a bale of hay a day, says Randa. It took several weeks for the gooey meat inspection sticker planted on her posterior to wear off.

Not long after Emily's story was carried by the wire service, featured in magazines and covered on national TV did the calls come from Hollywood.

"Ellen and Rob Little (from First Look Pictures) read about Emily in People Magazine and they called us. Three more producers contacted us too," says Randa. However, a number of factors worked into the Little's favor. "They're both vegetarians too -- longtime vegans even. And they also have a sanctuary in their home for animals. We felt that they would keep the integrity of Emily's story intact and further the cause of farm animals."

These "Hollywood" people break the stereotype of mass media exploitation some may have. "People should understand Emily's story will be in the film, not Emily. We don't want anything more to happen to this cow, " said Ellen Little, president of First Look Pictures.

Emily won't be traveling to California or any local sites used in filming. Rather, the cow in the film will be an amalgam or dummy or puppets, robotic cows and animal doubles. "Any animal used in the film will be placed in a permanent home," said Ellen Little, meaning no animal will be sent to a slaughterhouse after filming.

Part of the deal with the Littles also stipulated that proceeds from the film would be used to provide lifetime care for Emily. Not part of the deal but a sign of the Little's empathy for Emily was their decision to build her a barn. "It was just completed," says Randa of the $10,000 structure. "It gives her a secure area."

Randa says she's thrilled with the Little's approach. "We didn't want this done unless it was done right," she says. The Randas hope the film's a box office success, but the message of animal rights is what's foremost in their minds. "Emily knew what was going to happen to her," says Randa explaining why the cow bolted from the slaughterhouse. "She has an incredible will to live." A shot of adrenaline, Randa says, is what catapulted Emily over the fence.

The Littles were certainly impressed with Emily upon meeting her in Sherborn this summer. The Randas provided the introductions as Emily munched on a pile of hay. You almost expected the Littles to say to Emily, "Let's do lunch."

But being vegetarians the Littles opted to provide Emily with a lunch rather than anything more sinister and they actually got to meet her face to face. "She really is quite impressive and imposing when you are standing in front of her," said Rob Little, when the duo was in the region this summer.

Making a trip to Massachusetts to scout locations, retrace Emily's travels and see the MetroWest area, the Littles spent a week of recording the details of Emily's life.

And while this may seem farfetched for some, this is very much a reality. A Boston attorney negotiated the deal over several months for the Randas and First Look Pictures is no novice in the movie industry. Recent projects for the company include "Richard III", "The Secret of

Emily fooling around with Meg as Lewis and Abbey look
on. (Photo by Frank Veronsky of People Magazine)

Roan Inish", "Antonia's Line", (which took best foreign picture honors at this year's Academy Awards), and the recently released "The Big Squeeze."

The quiet barn that has become her home seems a million miles from the glamour normally associated with the movie industry but Emily, the cow that captured the imagination of many when she hopped out of a Hopkinton slaughterhouse nearly a year ago, is going Hollywood -- in a big way.

Don't expect too many more changes for this cow, though. Everything that will happen now to make the movie a reality will happen with Emily in mind, but not with Emily present.

Ellen Little said this week they are working to have as much of the movie made in Massachusetts and at MetroWest locations as is possible, but some scenes in almost every movie are done in a studio or on a soundstage. "The key here is that we want to shoot a movie faithful to Emily's story, without hurting any animal that is in the film," said Ellen Little.

What kind of story will that be? You can forget talking pigs and barnyard animals no matter how enchanting you may have found "Babe". Emily's story, for those who haven't followed the tale of the hefty heifer, is a holiday story (she "escaped" just before Thanksgiving and arrived at the Peace Abbey on Christmas Eve.)

"This will be a holiday movie. It is essentially a Christmas movie," said Little. First Look expects the movie to be ready in about a year, perhaps in time for the 1997 holiday movie season, and it will be distributed by a major domestic company, she said.

Emily the cow is now Emily the script and will soon be Emily the movie.

"It's just a great story," Little said. "A great story."

FROM INDIA TO EMILY WITH LOVE

By Amy Klein

SHERBORN With a handful of flowers and a splash of rice, four Hindu priests clad in yellow robes clustered around the stall to honor Emily, the 1400 pound cow.

"This is incredible," said Lewis Randa, keeper of the cow that made headlines last winter when she escaped death by running away from a slaughterhouse. "Emily's getting blessed in the Hindu tradition of the Sacred Cow. Could she be a reincarnated cow from India?"

Hearing about Emily's plight, Framingham resident Nityanand Patel and three Hindu disciples traveled from India, arriving last week to honor the cow – a sacred animal in the Hindu religion.

Emily's story has become famous to many Hindus, and one disciple said he read about the cow in an article in a South African newspaper.

"This is like meeting a famous person," said Jayenti Patel.

As the religious men scratched Emily's ears and fed her oats, they prayed to her as a holder of divine powers who has the ability to cleanse the mind, body and spirit.

"In Hinduism, the cow should be preserved at all costs," said Pranav Pandya, the chief priest and a doctor of scientific spirituality. It is Pandya's fifth trip to America, and this time he was determined to see the cow.

Emily's plight won the hearts of locals last winter when she escaped death by jumping the gate of the Arena Slaughterhouse and hiding out in the woods for 40 days. Lewis and Meg Randa finally found the cow Christmas Eve and bought her for $1. She now lives in the barn at the Peace Abbey.

Emily's story reflects many basic Hindu principles, particularly the avid opposition to slaughtering animals. Most practicing Hindus are vegetarians and believe that killing a cow is equivalent to killing a 'mother'.

While the priests were in Sherborn, they visited the Peace Abbey. Hindu philosophy is founded in non-violence, and the priests said they were thrilled with their first visit to a peace sanctuary.

"Nonviolence means not causing pain to anyone – not to a person nor to a cow," Pandya said.

Hindu Disciple/Priest Nityanand Patel applies red paint to Emily's forehead. (Photo by Ed Hopfmann, Middlesex News)

ANIMAL RIGHTS LEAP TO LIFE CREATES A "SPOKESCOW"

By Meenal Pandya

WELLESLEY   Emily, a 3-year-old Holstein cow, while being led into the killing room of a slaughterhouse in Hopkinton near here, suddenly broke free, jumped a five-foot gate at the edge of a loading dock on to the pavement and asphalt and ran into nearby woods, where she successfully eluded policemen and slaughterhouse hunters for 40 days.

She struggled through piles of snow and survived on a diet of frozen leaves, chestnuts and bales of hay left by an 'underground network' of Hopkinton's caring residents.

Luckily for her, Meg Randa who runs a Life Experience School in Sherborn with her husband Lewis Randa, read the news about Emily in the local newspaper. Driven by a desire to find the cow, Meg Randa started searching for her in the woods with her husband. Finally, they found Emily and brought her home after a struggle and paying $1 as a token price to the slaughterhouse owner, Frank Arena.

"You have to give her credit," says Meg Randa, a vegetarian. "She has to be an incredibly smart, determined cow to jump a five-foot gate out of the slaughterhouse building. Now we want to help her become a symbol and 'spokescow' to encourage people to stop eating meat."

Ever since the Randas had brought home Emily, she has become a celebrity. Several dozen well wishers come each day to pay a visit.

Lewis Randa, who as a vegetarian is ethically opposed not only to the practice of eating animals but also to the consumption of all dairy products, said he hopes Emily becomes the symbol of the "vegetarian movement".

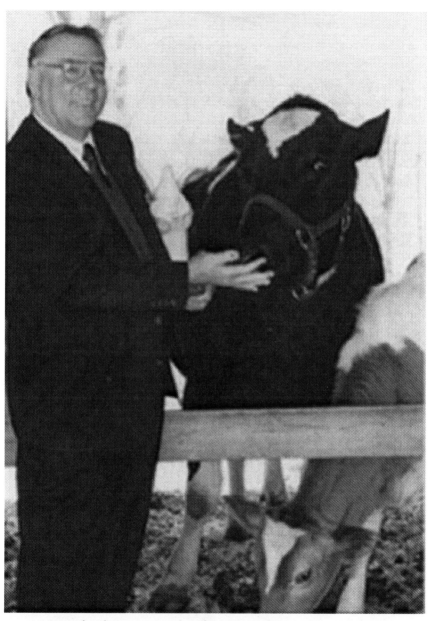

Animal rights activist and author, Howard Lyman, pays a visit to the Abbey barn to congratulate Emily for having been able to evade capture by slaughterhouse workers. (Photo by Lewis Randa)

"Emily will open the eyes of thousands of people to the cruel treatment of the dairy industry and the suffering these animals go through," he said.

Like the horses, goats, rabbits and dogs at Randa's Peace Abbey farm, Emily will be available to teach special needs children how to care for animals. Randa said that cows go through a lot of suffering. They are artificially inseminated to have calves and produce milk. The male babies are taken from them and killed for veal at a very young age. The mother cows are then milked for six to eight months and ultimately, when their milk production decreases are forced to produce another calf, only to have it taken from them. The cycle continues over and over again until this creature which has given its life, milk and off-spring is sent off to the slaughterhouse.

Before the Randa family came forward to buy this cow, two other Hopkinton residents, Ernest Clark and Bob Ahearn--both animal lovers -- had pledged to split a $500 cost of buying Emily and were determined to find her a home.

While Emily was hiding in the woods, the local paper ran a debate to find out "should Emily be turned over to the Randas or turned

Emily enjoying a summer day playing hide 'n seek with Meg behind tree to right.. (Photo by Lewis Randa)

into hamburger?", and, out of the 25 responses, only two respondents suggested the hamburger alternative. The owner of the slaughterhouse, Frank Arena, was so moved by the public support for Emily that he decided to sell the cow for only $1.

"If they can take care of her, they can have her," he said. The story of Emily has caught national attention and now Hollywood has purchased film rights to make a movie on Emily. She has stirred the debate about vegetarianism and given a face to the whole movement. "At least 50 people have come up to Emily and resolved to become vegetarian," says Meg Randa.

"To look Emily in the eye is to come face to face with someone who survived the killing floor of a slaughterhouse. Emily is here to serve as a teacher," says Lewis Randa, who only a year ago displeased his neighbors by erecting a statue of Mahatma Gandhi next to the War Memorial.

WALK-A-THON SUNDAY AT THE PEACE ABBEY

By Bonne Docherty

SHERBORN   Tomorrow will be a vegetarian's delight.

The Peace Abbey on Sunday will host a walk-a-thon for abandoned or abused farm animals, throw a vegetarian potluck supper, honor local farmers and dedicate a new barn for Emily the Cow.

The events start at noon with a five-kilometer walk to raise money for Farm Sanctuary. A bike-a-thon will begin at 1 p.m. at the Boston Marathon starting line in Hopkinton.

The Farm Sanctuary, which has shelters in New York and California, is like a humane society for farm animals.

It saves as many animals as it can from stockyards or overturned turkey trucks. It also fights for animal rights legislation and educates people about the plight of food animals, according to local volunteer Sara Martin-Pfister.

In addition to being a fund-raiser, this year's walk honors Emily, the cow who jumped over a gate at Hopkinton's Arena Slaughterhouse and escaped the butcher's blade.

Since December, she has lived at the Peace Abbey, which director Lewis Randa calls a "guest and retreat house for the peace movement".

When walkers and bikers convene at the Abbey around 2 p.m., the Boston Vegetarian Society's potluck supper will begin.

Randa will also present the Courage of Conscience award to Gene and Lori Bauston, co-founders of the Farm Sanctuary, and to Bill and Rose Abbot, founders of Hopkinton's Elmwood Farm, which grows fresh produce for the hungry.

Past recipients of the award include Gandhi, Mother Teresa, Rosa Parks, Muhammad Ali and Maya Angelou.

"The Baustons inspired us to get involved with giving sanctuary," Randa said. "And we have volunteered at the Abbotts. They empower people to act on the 'Sermon on the Mount'—to feed the hungry and care for the needy."

A new barn for Emily will be unveiled and blessed. The barn includes stalls for Emily and a companion and a vegetarian resource library.

Admission is free although non-walkers are encouraged to bring a vegan dish for six people or a contribution of $10.

Life is good. (Photo by Lewis Randa)

MILKIN' THIS ONE FOR ALL IT'S WORTH

Tom Moroney

"It's all a bunch of bull," said Frank Arena, slaughterhouse owner and former owner of Emily, the cow whose story is headed for Hollywood.

"I know the movie is going to be a (bleeping) slam against the meat industry," he grumbled.

If Arena sounds bitter and betrayed, who can blame the guy?

Right before Christmas last year, Emily the Cow defied death and hopped a fence at Arena's slaughterhouse in Hopkinton.

She was taken in by some eccentric vegetarians in Sherborn. And every cloven-hooved step of the way, her adventures were chronicled by some of our finest fact-gatherers here in this newsroom. Then came People Magazine and instant fame.

Now this big, walking warehouse of quarter-pounders is joining the ranks of Babe the Pig, Winnie the Pooh, and Don Knotts, who, as movie buffs will remember, once played a fish.

Arena says the Hollywood producers of Emily, who are vegetarians, have snubbed him. They haven't even bothered to pay him a visit, instead buying the rights to the Emily story from Sherborn celery-chompers Lew Randa and his wife.

True, the Randas did save Emily and put her up in their barn. True, Frank and his sons had something else in mind when Emily escaped. (They were going to shoot her.)

But if not for the Arenas, there would be no dramatic tension, no chance the star could have been lunch meat by now.

Here's another thing: Arena's 5-year-old granddaughter gave Emily her name. And the name is what helps make this movie so remarkable.

How enticing would this sound: Now playing in a theatre near you, Fred the Cow?

"I think we should get something, even if it's just a little nest egg my grand daughter can put away for her college education," Arena said.

I called the movie producers, but they were in Europe and unreachable. Perhaps word reached them that I, too, would like to see Emily turned into roast beef dinner, with a side of roast potatoes.

It's a great story, don't get me wrong. I even talked to the Randas once about writing something myself.

But together Emily fever is a true epidemic that moves with the speed of hoof-and-mouth disease.

A cow lover posting her thoughts on the Internet compares Emily's escape from Arena's slaughterhouse and consequent meanderings to those of Christ and his 40 nights in the desert. Bovine as messiah figure.

Is that what they mean by cheeseburgers in paradise?

After Emily eluded execution and settled into her new Sherborn sanctuary, she's even written a column or two published in these pages and adorned with her headshot, although the writing itself, I suspect, was done by Randa.

By the way, he's a founder of something called the Sherborn Peace Abbey, which hands out peace trophies to famous peaceniks like. Well, I forget.

Am I jealous? Extremely. I had my sights set on a career path much like the cows: first a column and then Hollywood.

Yet, this is more than jealousy at work. Talking to Arena, I got the distinct feeling that Hollywood is missing the big picture. Emily, as it turns out, is not the first animal to escape.

Ten years ago, a bull got loose and made its way seven miles from Hopkinton to Rte.9 in Framingham. The police called Frank. He went down, took a shot with his rifle and missed.

Then the police took a few shots and didn't miss. The bull jumped into the nearby reservoir, showing up a few days later, washed up dead on the other side of the reservoir.

Three years later, a mean and nasty bull got loose and had to be brought down by a deer slug. The police had fired several shots from their .357 Magnum "but those bullets went into the Bull's head and got flattened like a pancake," Arena recalled.

See what I'm getting at here? Emily is the first to get over Arena's fence and live. That puts her story among the greatest prison bust-outs of all time.

Forget the cow as messiah figure. I like this plot line much better: Cow as Clint Eastwood.

TALK BACK TO TOM

Reader will bear gifts

Hello Tom. Regarding your column on Sunday Oct. 27, "Milking this one for all it's worth," You seem rather misinformed on the subject of vegetarianism. "Celery chompers" and "eccentric" are not the words I would use to describe the many vegetarians I know. Educated and compassionate would be more accurate. The Arenas and their abattoir represent pain, misery, disease, and death. Why would Hollywood want to talk with him? There's an abundance of violence in movies already. The Randas and The Peace Abbey you've belittled represent courage, conviction, compassion, and hope. Qualities we all need more of. Your quotes, calling Emily the cow a "big walking warehouse of quarter-pounders" and that you would like to see Emily "turned into a roast beef dinner, with a side of potatoes," have shown me your brutal and childish nature. Is that what you were trying to convey in writing this column. I promise to visit you in the coronary care unit, bearing gifts of celery to chomp, if you'll print my reply.

J.C. Maynard

People Magazine photographer Jeff Olson gives
Emily her favorite treat, a N.Y. bagel.
(Photo: Ed Hopfmann, Middlesex News)

HOW ABOUT A S-MOO-CH
EMILY HAS A KISS, THEN A BEEF
WITH PHOTOGRAPHERS

By Patrick McGee

SHERBORN   Back for their second article, *People Magazine* photographers were given a scare yesterday when they were chased by Emily, the sacred cow of MetroWest, revered for her escaped from the slaughterhouse almost a year ago.

Still "feisty," Emily charged the two photographers in hopes of drawing them into some playful cowing around, said Meg Randa, the cow's caregiver.

Fearing a mad cow, one photographer dashed on top of a stone wall, while another hid behind a tree.

The two had driven from New York City to see the courageous cow that escaped a slaughterhouse.

The photographers, Frank Veronsky and Jeff Olson, befriended Emily by treating her to some of their New York bagels. They walked out of the barn at the end of their shoot and the cow's feast, but Emily decided the fun wasn't over.

Veronsky, Olson and Randa looked behind them to discover, Holy Cow! They were being chased by a 1,400 pound beast!

"Before I knew it she came charging down the hill, threw her head down, kicked up her heels and scattered everybody," Randa said. "Emily was just enjoying all the attention."

Randa said the 3-year-old cow wasn't being aggressive, only playful. Randa and her husband Lewis, director of the Peace Abbey in Sherborn, took in the cow after it escaped from the Arena Slaughterhouse on Nov. 14, 1995.

Richie Balanca, one of Emily's special caregivers from the Life Experience School. (Photo by Lewis Randa)

HAPPY ENDINGS:
PUTTING A FACE ON MEAT

Emily the Cow loves life. This comes as no revelation to those who already know that cows are sensitive, self aware, unique individuals. But for many, the story of Emily's fight for life has been a spiritual awakening.

Emily is really no different from the millions of dairy cows who are slaughtered once their output wanes. She was headed for a violent death when she arrived at the slaughterhouse in Hopkinton, Massachusetts, on November 14, 1995. Like the other frightened cows, Emily sensed the horror that lay ahead, but rather than succumb in confused and helpless terror, she propelled all 1,400 pounds of herself over a 5-foot-high gate and escaped into the surrounding woods.

Reminiscent of a Biblical odyssey, for 40 days and 40 nights this courageous cow eluded her captors, enduring severe snowstorms and freezing temperatures, all the while foraging for sustenance. Local media began chronicling the Holstein's plight, prompting sympathizers to leave secret stashes of hay in backyards and woods. When vegetarians Meg and Lewis Randa heard about Emily, they contacted the slaughterhouse owner who offered to sell the brave bovine to them for $1. Then on Christmas Eve, after days of trying, the Randas finally coaxed a frightened but tired Emily into a trailer for the ride to the sanctuary at The Peace Abbey, a part of the Randas' school for children with special needs.

Now settled into her new home, tender loving care has done wonders for Emily, who is now back up to 1,800 pounds after losing 500 pounds during her fugitive days. Lewis Randa says that Emily is contented and at peace, and despite her ordeals at the hands of humans, she prefers the company of people to her animal companions.

Emily's influence and circle of friends continues to grow. Hundreds of well-wishers have come to visit the now-famous cow. She welcomes a good head scratch, loves carrots and other treats offered from outstretched palms, and freely gives away kisses in the form of a giant lick. Her effect on people is powerful: many swear off red meat or become vegetarian after meeting her. She has even been a 'bridesmaid' at a wedding held in the Abbey barn.

Serving as a compelling ambassador for vegetarianism, Emily has garnered national media attention, including a full-page profile in People Magazine. A motion picture about Emily's story is in the works.

Why have people been so moved by one cow's courageous effort to avoid death? Perhaps it's because for the first time, they see that "meat" has a face.

EMILY GETS A NEW BARN

By Bonnie Docherty

SHERBORN   Almost one year after escaping from a local slaughterhouse, Emily the Cow has a barn of her own, complete with easy chairs, an antique barber's chair, and a TV with VCR.

"She loves it in here," said 14-year-old Bud Lench, whose father, Larry, built the barn. The barn, located at the Peace Abbey and Life Experience School, also serves as a vegetarian resource center.

Emily inspecting her new home: a barn built just for her by movie producers Ellen and Rob Little. (Photo by Frank Veronsky of People Magazine)

"The barn is an educational center and Emily's the main teacher," said director Lewis Randa, who described to Peace Abbey as a guest and retreat house for the peace movement.

Emily, a 3-year-old Holstein, jumped over the gate out of the Hopkinton's Arena Slaughterhouse last November and escaped the butcher's blade. After roaming free for more than a month, she was caught and found a permanent safe haven with the Randas, who don't eat meat or consume dairy products.

Her story attracted national attention, including an article in People Magazine.

First Look Pictures plans to make a movie about her adventures, and executive producers Ellen and Rob Little paid for the $10,000 barn and a supply of hay.

"The (movie) contract is written so Emily will be taken care of for the rest of her life," Randa said.

The barn was designed by Randa and his wife, Meg. Attached to the old barn Emily shared with her horse friend, Shoshone, her new home includes a stall with plenty of room for a 1,400 pound bovine.

When visitors come in, the friendly cow leans her nose over the railing looking for a treat and human contact. She loves people.

"It's wonderful people can be in the barn with her," Meg Randa said of the living room next to the stall.

The barn is decorated with cow flags and bumper stickers such as "friends don't let friends drink milk". Newspaper articles about her escapades cover one wall. A sign on the wall urges a 'yes' vote on Tuesday's Question 1 on the ballot which would prohibit steel jaw and the padded steel jaw leg hold traps.

When she's not licking the chair backs, Emily likes to stick her nose in the grocery cart of vegetarian food alternatives, such as Rice Dream (similar to ice cream), and Breakfast Strips, a non-meat bacon substitute

"It's a chance for people to learn more about vegetarianism," Meg Randa said. "We're not here to force our beliefs on people or push them down their throats. We're just explaining alternatives."

A library of vegetarian cookbooks and information about animal rights lines the walls of the human part of the barn. Videos on the subject are also available for viewing.

The animal rights movement is basically the Golden Rule applied to animals as well as people, Lewis Randa said. "We don't want to be chased, bitten, eaten by animals so we should apply the same rule to how we relate to animals in return" he continued.

The Randas became vegetarians about three years ago and stopped using dairy products six month before Emily arrived, Meg said.

"I expected Emily to be a beef cow," she said. "When I saw that she was a black and white Holstein, I understood the connection between dairy cows and the meat industry. Holsteins are generally milk cows, but they are probably the main source of hamburger meat."

Since moving into her new home about two weeks ago, Emily has had a constant stream of visitors.

"A Catholic came in and kneeled down to confess to Emily, and said "I will not eat animals again, "said Lench, a student at the Life Experience School. A confessional is placed right next to her stall.

HOLY COW!

It's worshipped as a god after escaping from slaughterhouse

James McCandish

Emily - an amazing black and white Holstein heifer -- jumped a gate and escaped from a slaughterhouse. And now Hindus are coming from as far away as India to worship her!

"She's incredible," said Lewis Randa, Emily's owner. "She saved her own life by fleeing the slaughterhouse, then survived 40 days and 40 nights foraging in 18 inches of snow with the deer in nearby woods."

"She lost 500 pounds before we found her and brought her home on Christmas Eve."

"Now people from all over the world are finding inspiration in her story."

In August, a chief Hindu priest and three disciples traveled from India -- where cows are considered sacred -- to Massachusetts to pay homage to the astonishing creature.

They bowed and prayed to her as a holder of divine powers that has the ability to cleanse the mind, body and spirit.

They showered her with flowers and rice, scratched her ears and fed her oats.

"In Hinduism the cow should be preserved at all costs," said chief priest Pranay Pandya, a doctor of scientific spirituality. "Emily is definitely special."

Emily, 4, was in a holding pen awaiting the killing floor at the Arena slaughterhouse in Hopkinton, Mass, last November 14, when she made her dramatic flight to freedom.

As the other animals were being led to slaughter, the alert 1,400 pound cow bounded over a five-foot metal gate and off a four-foot dock. Then she ran for her life.

On December 19, Meg Randa read about Emily's odyssey in a local newspaper and rushed to the rescue.

"We are vegetarians, pacifists, and interested in animal rights," explained Randa of Sherborn, Mass.

"We couldn't bear the thought of this poor cow out in the woods in sub-zero temperatures starving to death."

For several days the Randas and their three children tracked Emily in the snow. When they found her, they won her confidence by feeding her grain and warm water. Finally they were able to lead her to a trailer -- and bring her home.

"We paid the slaughterhouse $1 for her. By this time she had lost 500 pounds and wasn't much use for hamburger," said the animal lover.

Back at the Randa's barn, word spread quickly about Emily and she became a celebrity. People from all over the U.S began visiting her and now she's back up to a prime 1,400 pounds.

"She'll live like a queen for the rest of her life," vowed Randa, 'surrounded by warmth, love, and devotees inspired by her story."

EMILY: 1 YEAR AS A FREE COW
Tabloids highlight anniversary

By Bonnie Docherty

SHERBORN   Holy Cow!

On the anniversary of her escape from a Hopkinton slaughterhouse, Emily the cow has truly become a national celebrity.

She is featured in this week's National Enquirer along with O.J Simpson, J.F.K Jr, and the British royal family.

Lewis Randa, keeper of the 1,400 pound bovine, said he was surprised about the Enquirer article because he was never interviewed for the story which quoted him several times. Most of the information was taken from Middlesex News articles.

But the story has helped spread the Peace Abbey's message about cruelty to animals and the importance of vegetarianism.

"We've received wonderful letters from National Enquirer readers, many of whom are animal lovers," Randa said. "We definitely would have avoided the paper, but its readers eat three meals a day, too."

The article coincides with the first anniversary of Emily's escape.

Last Nov. 14, the 3-year-old Holstein escaped the butcher's blade by jumping a five-foot fence at Hopkinton's Arena Slaughterhouse. Neighbors put out hay for the fugitive, and the Arenas agreed to sell her for $1 to Randa and his wife, Meg.

After roaming free for more than a month, Emily was caught and moved to a permanent safe haven at the Sherborn Peace Abbey on Christmas Eve.

The Randas, who run the Peace Abbey, are both vegans -- people who don't eat meat or consume dairy products.

The Enquirer article, accompanied by color photos, tells the story of the Hopkinton Holstein. Headlined "Holy Cow! It's worshipped as a god after escaping from slaughterhouse," it focuses on a visit from Hindu priests in August.

The priests came from India to honor the cow, whose reputation has spread across the globe. Cows are sacred animals in the Hindu religion.

The Hindus' visit was just one of many highlights in Emily's first year of freedom.

On Jan. 14, family and friends gathered at the Peace Abbey to celebrate the two-month anniversary of her escape.

Later that month, she appeared in a People Magazine article profiled in "A Profile in Cowrage."

First Look Pictures, which produced Oscar-winner "Antonia's Line", recently announced that it plans to make a movie about the cow's adventures. Proceeds from the movie will help care for Emily.

Executive producers Ellen and Rob Little also spent $10,000 on a new barn for their star. The barn includes a living room with easy chairs, a TV and VCR and a library about animal rights.

Meg Randa telling the story of Emily's escape from
the slaughterhouse and her new mission
to touch the hearts of people who visit The Peace Abbey.
(Photo by Stephen Tackeff, Middlesex News)

Emily moved in a couple weeks ago and is enjoying both her new abode and the steady stream of admirers that come to visit.

Not a bad year for a cow that barely escaped becoming ground beef.

And to celebrate her journey from Hopkinton to home to Hollywood, the Randas and other friends of Emily will bike today from the Arena Slaughterhouse to the Peace Abbey.

DOES THE BIBLE CALL FOR A VEGETARIAN DIET?

By George R. Plagenz

So far it is only beef that has British meat eaters nervous in the wake of the outbreak of the fatal "mad cow disease" believed to be linked to beef cattle.

Beef has disappeared from the dinner fare of England's top hostesses. According to one British newspaper account, Lady Melchett said, "I wouldn't dream of giving beef to my guests." She recently served guinea fowl instead of beef.

If British housewives are passing up steaks and roasts at the butcher shop, some people are beginning to wonder whether lamb chops and baked ham will be next to get the cold shoulder in view of the possible harmful effects of the chemicals in most animal diets.

The idyllic picture of cattle munching sweet, fresh grass in the meadow is more like something out of pastoral poetry and song than a sight you will see motoring along the rural roads of Hereford or Iowa today.

Might it not be the better part of wisdom, cautious cooks are asking, to move to a diet of vegetables and grains?

Vegetarians have always been with us of course. Our earliest ancestors were probably vegetarians.

The Genesis account of creation suggests that God intended for all mankind to be herbivorous. "And God Said, 'Behold, I have given you every plant that yields seed that is upon the face of the earth, and every tree whose fruit yields seed: it be to you for food.'"(Genesis 1:29).

There have been vegetarians throughout history who have refused to eat meat on religious or moral grounds that had their origins in these verses from Genesis.

Fr. Bruce Williams blesses Emily in the pasture as part of the animal blessing ceremony on the Feast of St. Francis of Assisi. (Photo by Lewis Randa)

Vegetarians have included Socrates, Plato, da Vinci, Einstein, Mahatma Gandhi, John Milton, Robert Cummings, Gloria Swanson and George Bernard Shaw. Shaw, who lived to be 94, became a vegetarian are age 25 after reading to lines of Percy Shelley's poetry: Never again may blood of bird or beast/ Stain with its venomous stream a human feast!

An early spiritualist, Helen Blavatsky, told how on one occasion as she was coming into Chicago on a train "a profound sense of desolation" oppressed her spirit.

"This of course has happened to others as they have approached Chicago," wryly observed author Gerald Carson in relating the story. But in this instance Mrs. Blavatsky was able to search out a theosophical basis for her melancholy. She was getting astral messages -- vibrations -- from the thousands of slaughtered beasts in Chicago's slaughterhouses.

Mrs. Blavatsky embraced vegetarianism at that moment.

Ellen White, a leading Seventh-day Adventist of the late 19th century, made vegetarianism a major tenet of her faith. It remains so today. One of the reasons for her rejection of meat is that meat contains toxic substances not found in vegetables and grains, she said.

This is the reason given for the return to meatless (or at least beefless) meals today in Britain.

EMILY HAS A NEW COMPANION

By Harry R. Weber

SHERBORN   Emily the cow met Belle the goat yesterday for a Thanksgiving Day feast of spinach and pumpkin pie, corn and nuts.

The meatless celebration at the Peace Abbey in Sherborn was intended to promote vegetarianism and make a statement about keeping animals from the slaughterhouse. Meg and Lewis Randa, the pacifists

Belle the Goat jumped off a truck in the parking lot of the same slaughterhouse from which Emily escaped. (Photo by Meg Randa)

Thanksgiving at the Peace Abbey ... two turkeys named Giving and Thanks and Belle the Goat enjoy dinner. Emily the Cow was brought in a few minutes later due to her ability to eat so much so fast. (Photo by Stephen Tackeff)

and vegetarians who run the Abbey, introduced Belle, their newest addition, to the world.

"This holiday is about being thankful and about giving," said 7-year old Abbey Randa in a speech she and her brother, Mike, prepared. "I've been a vegetarian for a year because I love animals."

Said 9-year-old Mike Randa: "Today is my anniversary of becoming a vegetarian. I saw a turkey on the table and I knew I didn't want to eat them anymore."

Belle, a 5-year-old American Alpine goat, jumped off a truck and escaped from a slaughterhouse three weeks ago, and a woman who found the animal gave it to the Randas. Emily, meanwhile, has been with the Randas since last Christmas Eve, which was six weeks after the cow escaped from the Arena Slaughterhouse in Hopkinton.

"This is the first time they've met," said Lewis Randa, as Emily reached her long neck underneath the stall and kissed Belle.

The Randas say they have promoted Emily and Belle to increase awareness of the cruelty of eating animal flesh.

Many news organizations, including People Magazine and the National Enquirer, have written about Emily. A Hollywood film producer plans to make a movie about the cow's escapade. The Randas said several people have suggested to the film producer that former Beatles member Paul McCartney write a song for the movie. (The land the Peace Abbey sits on was paid for in part by a donation from Yoko Ono, wife of the late Beatles member John Lennon).

Despite all the hoopla made over Emily, the Randas insist they are taking care of the cow and Bell and goat for a worthy cause. They are members of the organization called People for the Ethical Treatment of Animals and have been vegetarians for four years.

Frank Arena, owner of the slaughterhouse from which Emily escaped, said he believes the Randas are publicity seekers. "This thing is crazy. It's been blown all out of proportion."

"The Peace Abbey is a place for the coming together of the different religions of the world," said Meg Randa, wearing an apron emblazoned with a picture of Emily.

Said Lewis Randa: "(Emily's) value is that she tweaks at people's conscience. That's a good thing."

MOO-O-VE OVER, BABE, FOR EMILY

Hollywood comes calling for Sherborn's famous runaway

By Doreen Iudica Vigue

SHERBORN Last year, she was the Cow that Came for Christmas. This year, she is the Holstein headed for Hollywood. Emily the Cow, a 3-year-old, black-and-white heifer who lives at the Peace Abbey here, is perhaps the most beloved bovine this side of Bombay.

Her story made international headlines last December after she escaped from a Hopkinton slaughterhouse by doing what no cow there had done before: She hurled her 1,400 pounds of choice cuts over a 5-foot holding gate and disappeared into the woods.

After being on the lam for 40 days and 40 nights, Emily was wooed to safety on Christmas Eve by the Randa family, pacifists and animal-rights activists who saw Emily's leap to freedom as the beginning of a spiritual and symbolic journey.

They brought her to their compound in the middle of town, where they run a spiritual retreat center and a school for disabled children. Each year since 1988, Meg and Lewis Randa have bestowed a Courage of Conscience Aware on people who work for peace. World-renowned luminaries such as Mother Teresa, the Dalai Lama and Muhammad Ali have received the honor.

Emily couldn't have asked to be in better company, or in a safer haven. The larger-than-life-sized statue of Gandhi she can see from her barn also assures her she's in the right place.

Now, Emily's true and touching tale is about to become, well, a mooovie.

*Randa cousins, Mikey, Davey, Abbey, Chris, Danny, and Jessica Randa
with Emily flossing her teeth on Abbey's hair! (Photo by Lewis Randa)*

First Look Pictures, a motion picture distribution company, has purchased the rights to the Emily saga and has begun work on the screenplay. Ellen Little, who heads First Look, discovered Emily on the pages of People magazine and decided the story of her escape was so magical that it deserved to be on the silver screen.

"Emily's spirit and the human beings in the community who came to her rescue and who were touched by her make a heartwarming, beautiful story," said Little, who is hoping that Emily becomes as big a box-office hit as "Babe"

Little hopes to begin filming on location soon, and would like the movie to be in theaters by next Christmas.

Emily has already gotten the star treatment. Little paid for the construction of a $10,000 barn for the cow -- complete with TV and VCR -- and pledged a lifetime endowment to her.

A film crew from London was at the barn Friday to film a segment about Emily for an English television show and a Japanese camera crew is also planning a visit.

Last winter, Emily was a bridesmaid at the wedding of a vegetarian couple who vowed in the barn to love, honor and forsake all steaks.

"She's become a spokescow for vegetarianism," said Lewis Randa, explaining that he and his wife Meg are vegans, the strictest of vegetarians who don't eat or wear or use animal products. "People meet Emily and never want to eat meat again."

In August, a group of Hindu priests traveled from India to the Abbey to honor Emily, the holy cow. They showered her with flowers, fed her oats, and as they sat cross-legged on the floor of her stall, prayed to her as a holder of divine powers.

The Randas and other Emily fans firmly believe that her life was spared by divine intervention. A major boost of adrenaline didn't hurt, either.

She made her leap to freedom on Nov. 14, 1995, just moments before she was to be herded into a slaughter room at the A. Arena & Sons slaughterhouse.

For weeks, slaughterhouse workers and police officers tried to find her. To the Arena people, she was $500 worth of hamburger roaming free. To authorities, she was a ton of trouble, running through backyards and even down Main Street. There was talk of shooting her to prevent anyone from being injured.

As almost daily reports in the Middlesex News chronicled cow sightings, residents began to take pity on her, a sentiment that only grew when she was christened "Emily" by the granddaughter of the slaughterhouse owner. Sympathizers soon stopped calling police when they saw the cow, and began leaving food for her in their backyards.

"People had a lot of respect for this cow, for the strength and courage she showed," said Meg Randa, 40. "They didn't look at her and think "dinner", they looked at her and thought "survivor"".

After reading about Emily for the first time on Dec. 19, Meg Randa was smitten: She had to catch that cow. The next day, the Randas offered slaughterhouse owner Frank Arena $500 for her. Arena initially said that $350 seemed like a fair price, since Emily probably had lost about 500 pounds.

But, caught up in the Christmas spirit, Arena thought better of the big bucks and told the Randas that Emily could be theirs for just $1 -- if they could find her.

"We just felt that if they wanted her that much, they could have her," said Joanne Arena, the slaughterhouse clerk. "We never regretted our decision. We want her to have a nice life."

The couple set out the next day, combing the woods of Hopkinton by the slaughterhouse in thigh-high snow, following what they thought were cow hoof tracks and leaving behind a trail of grain. It took several days of searching in the cold, but the couple would not be cowed.

They spotted Emily a few miles from the slaughterhouse on the morning of Christmas Eve, won her trust with food, loving strokes and whispered words of encouragement and lured her into a trailer for the ride to her new home.

On Christmas, the family ate a vegetarian dinner by her stall, allowing her to gobble everything in the breadbasket.

Home for Emily is now Strawberry Fields, the compound where the Randas run the Greater Boston Vegetarian Resource Center and the 25-year-old Life Experience School for disabled children and the Peace Abbey.

Since her rescue, the excitement surrounding Emily has barely abated.

Meg Randa wrote a children's book about Emily in the cow's own "voice", and the couple is working with the founders of an animal sanctuary in New York to create "the Peaceable Kingdom", an animal-rights peace memorial to be located in the Los Angeles area.

The Randas have relocated the Vegetarian Resource Center to Emily's barn, which is full of animal-rights and vegetarian literature and has velvet chairs and a sofa for visitors.

And Emily gets new visitors every day, including a family last week who included her in their family Christmas card photo. People from all over the world still send cards, letters and emails.

"Our feeling from the beginning was it was all pre-destined by a higher power," said Meg Randa. "It restores my belief that life is full of gifts and that God works in mysterious ways -- even with cows."

JOLLY GOOD SHOW FOR EMILY

In this episode, the cow gets filmed for British TV

By Bonnie Docherty

SHERBORN   From Hopkinton to Hollywood to London. Emily the cow's fame has spread across the ocean and she will soon make a special appearance on the British TV program "The Fortean Times".

And American crew hired by Rapido, the British company that produces the show, filmed Emily Friday with her "family", friends and faithful followers.

"I love her and the whole place," said free-lance producer Terri Taylor, who was part of the film crew.

The feeling was mutual. Emily nuzzled and licked Taylor during much of the filming.

Emily escaped death and garnered fame last year when she leapt over the fence of Hopkinton's Arena Slaughterhouse. After wandering in the woods for about five weeks, she was caught by Meg and Lewis Randa, who bought her for $1 from slaughterhouse owner Frank Arena and gave her a home at the Peace Abbey.

Since then, First Look Pictures has started work on a holiday film about the runaway Holstein, and the media has spread her story around the world.

English TV producers read about Emily in the National Enquirer, which published an article on the anniversary of her escape.

"After the mad cow disease (in Britain), we thought it was well worth having Emily's story covered," said Meg Randa, who added that the Brits have an active animals rights movement.

Hindu Disciple/Priest Nityanand Patel and Nagin Patel with Emily. (Photo by Ed Hopfmann, Middlesex News)

Taylor and her crew began the day at the Arena slaughterhouse. The Arenas declined an interview and called the police, Taylor said. The film crew then left.

At the Peace Abbey, Meg Randa told the filmmakers how she read about Emily in the Middlesex News and, with her family, decided to bring the cow home.

"I felt a very special connection (when I first saw her)," Randa said. "She ran away, then circled back and came right up to me."

Since she was brought to the Peace Abbey last Christmas, Emily has been visited by monks from Cambodia, Hindu priests from India and Rosemary Von Trapp of "The Sound of Music" fame, Randa told Taylor.

One of the highlights of the film will be a Hindu ceremony in which Emily is showered with rice and flower petals. Hindu priest Nityanand Patel painted Emily's forehead with red paint and chanted prayers -- four times for the camera.

"A miracle saved Emily," Patel said. "She's a message from the Almighty to people. It is a message against cruelty to animals and the message of vegetarianism."

Patel said he thinks Emily is special not only because she is a cow, which is a sacred animal for Hindus. She also escaped on Nehru's birthday (Nov. 14), wandered for 40 days and 40 nights like Jesus did, and was caught on Christmas Eve, "an auspicious occasion," Patel said.

"Lord Krishna loves the cow," said one of the several Hindus who attended the ceremony.

Emily loved the attention and particularly the food. In fact she seemed more porcine than bovine.

She "pigged out" on apples, bread and rice and "hammed" it up with film crew.

"She's relishing my cuisine," Patel said, who was also a bit of a ham. When Taylor said she had all the footage she needed, Patel said he was "pumped up" for more.

After the religious rituals were finished, Patel gave his audience a geography lesson.

The white mark on Emily's forehead is shaped like India, and Patel pointed out Madras, Bombay, Calcutta and Delhi.

The film crew also taped a daily ritual at the Randas' Life Experience School, a peace school for children with disabilities.

The 11 children dipped their fingers in a bowl of water, recited an incantation to "Brother Sun" and "Sister Moon", and honored the 12 major religions.

"Emily teaches us morals. And she is very, very fun," said student Bud Lench, 14.

After about five minutes of filming, the crew had to leave for an appointment in Boston.

"The Fortean Times" normally does shows about "strange occurrences and psychic connections," Taylor said.

Her next assignment was to film an artist who says he was abducted by aliens. The aliens, he claims, put a metal plate on his head which they use to transmit ideas for his paintings.

"Does he do still life or landscapes?" asked Meg Randa.

Taylor promised to get back to her on that.

HOLY COW! SHE'S A HOLSTEIN HERO

With one big leap for Bovinekind, Emily fled her fate as a roast to become a meatless role model

If it were a children's story, it would stretch credibility. But occasionally, fairy tales do come true. This one began in November 1995, when a seemingly ordinary cow was lined up outside A. Arena & Sons, a Hopkinton, Mass slaughterhouse. In a gravity-defying bid to escape, the

Emily and Meg are centerfold in People Magazine.
(Photo by Frank Veronsky of People Magazine)

1,400-pound heifer jumped a five-foot gate and headed for the woods. To the bemusement of town folks and the chagrin of the company and the constabulary, she eluded capture, living hoof-to-mouth for more than a month. Eventually, ardent vegetarians Meg and Lewis Randa, who run a small school for children with special needs, bought the cow called Emily for $1 and lured her to safety with buckets of grain.

Emily, 4, now lives high on the hay on the Peace Abbey grounds in Sherborn, Mass. A celebrity of sorts, she is, says Meg, 40 "an ambassador of compassion for animals." Emily frequently receives mail from fans who say, "I used to eat meat, but because of you, I don't anymore." A group of Hindu priests from India, believing she is perhaps the reincarnation of a sacred cow, paused in their recent tour of the U.S. to place a red caste mark on her forehead. She's also a hot Hollywood property. Producer Ellen Little of First Look Pictures bought the film rights to Emily's saga for a sum Randa estimates "will provide Emily with food, veterinary care, housing and companionship for the rest of her life." Little also donated $10,000 for a new barn which includes an attached educational center, chock-full of books and other information about vegetarianism and animal rights. Not a bad deal considering Emily won't have to lift a hoof in the planned feature. As befits a star of her, um, magnitude, she will have a body double.

"She's probably the most well-known cow in the world," says owner Meg Randa

FORMER FUGITIVE COW BECOMES VEGETARIANS' #1 SYMBOL

By Don Seiffert

We all know the cow is news. But how did Emily, probably Sherborn's most famous current resident, become the patron saint of vegetarians?

Since being brought to the Sherborn Peace Abbey just over a year ago, hundreds have come to visit her, says owner Meg Randa. Of those, she said that easily 50 of those, whom she knows, have either become vegetarians or cut out some meat from their diet.

Now that the news of an upcoming movie has put Emily the Cow in national headlines (including, ironically, "People" magazine), even more people have come to pay their respects to her.

The Randas, Meg and her husband Lewis have even made up a New Year's resolution checklist for visitors that lists various kinds of animal products to stop using.

Although there have been a couple of dramatic conversions to vegetarianism, more often Emily acts as a catalyst for people who may have been considering becoming a vegetarian, effectively giving a face to the hamburger you eat for lunch, and a voice to the steak you eat for dinner.

"Emily's presence has an effect on people," said Meg. After seeing her, people "feel like Emily's looking over their shoulder every time they eat", she said.

Emily first made headlines following her escape from a Hopkinton slaughterhouse in November, 1995. She jumped a 5 foot gate just moments before she was going to be killed.

When Meg heard about her daring escape in the news, she contacted the owner of the slaughterhouse about buying the cow. After almost

Emily in her new barn, a gift from Ellen and Rob Little, film producers from Los Angeles. (Photo by Frank Veronsky of People Magazine)

six weeks of being out in the snowy forest on her own, Emily allowed herself to be lured by hay, sweet grains, warm water and good measure of tugging.

"She was able to stay alive in the forest by digging a hole in which to keep warm," Meg said. Meg said she couldn't say if Emily was in fact smarter than the average cow, because she'd never had a cow before Emily.

"She's incredibly tuned into her environment," she said.

Lewis and Meg Randa are themselves vegans, and avoid all animal products, including dairy products and eggs. In addition to the Peace Abbey and a small school, they have established the Vegetarian Resource Center, with a collection of literature and recipes of vegetarian dishes.

Lewis Randa said that they became vegetarians about four years ago when a friend asked offhandedly if they were vegetarians.

Lewis said their response was, " no, but we know we should be." They decided then to cut meat out of their diet, and later became vegans.

In addition, now they don't wear leather, silk, or wool, all byproducts of the slaughterhouse.

Although most people can understand, though they may not agree with, the moral reasoning behind not eating meat, the idea of cutting out animal products that can be obtained without directly killing the animal is just too much a stretch for many.

But for the Randas, it is the logical next step.

Lewis said that the milk industry supports the veal industry because milk that would normally go to calves is instead sold, while the calves are fed an iron-deficient diet. Similarly, he claimed that the wool industry economically supports the lamb industry.

Their concern for living things ranges down to the insect world. Lewis said that silk is made by boiling live silkworm cocoons, and Meg added that commercial beekeepers often kill many of their bees in the process of making honey. They therefore avoid such products as well.

Emily's presence embodies their belief in non-violence, and, said Meg, reinforces their own and dozens of others' commitments to reduce cruelty to animals.

ONE COW, ONE TROPHY, GREAT NEWS!

Animal rights group cites Emily coverage for cherished award

By Carol Beggy

First, Emily, the fence-jumping, slaughterhouse evading cow, went Hollywood, now she's taking MetroWest with her.

An international animal rights group has chosen the Middlesex News to receive a trophy for the paper's coverage of the wayward cow since her escape more than a year ago.

Other's recognized include the movie "Fly Away Home," television show "Ellen," news magazine "Date-Line NBC," the PBS children's series "Kratt's Creatures," and the Discovery Channel's documentary "The Free Willy Story: Keiko's Journey Home".

The Ark Trust announced the 19 recipients of the 11th annual Genesis Awards this week, naming the Middlesex News as the print category winner "for spotlighting animal issues with courage, creativity and integrity." Previous winners in this category include the Los Angeles Times, The Village Voice, and the New York Times Magazine. The News is the only newspaper in New England to win this award and is the smallest daily newspaper so honored.

Specifically cited by the trust were News reporter Rodney Schussler, who broke the cow story, and former Bureau Chief, Carolyn Fretz.

"While size of the audience reached by a story is often a factor, the judges realized (the Middlesex News) had committed a lot of resources to this story and had made a commitment to covering the story," said Lisa Agabian, public information manager for the Trust.

"It isn't always easy for news organizations to tell these stories and that's even more the case with smaller outlets," Agabian said.

Middlesex News Editor Andrea Haynes noted the Emily story was the product of many people in all of the paper's editorial departments, but pointed to the determined reporting of Schussler as significant for putting the cow's story in the national headlines.

"Without Rodney's persistence when he heard about the cow who jumped out of the slaughterhouse, Emily might not have survived to become the famous symbol she is today," Haynes said. "One of the

Special to the Middlesex News -- News reporter Rodney Schussler talks to presenter Linda Blair backstage after receiving his award for coverage of Emily the Cow during the 11th Annual Genesis Awards Ceremony at the Century Plaza Hotel in Los Angeles, California. (AP Photo, Middlesex News, Ken McGagh)

strengths of the Middlesex News is its commitment to following stories. I'm pleased this prestigious award recognizes that ability."

All 1996 Genesis Awards were selected from material released in 1996. Entries are submitted by those in the industry or by "people's choice", with finalists voted upon by the 19-member Genesis Awards Committee. The News' entry was submitted by Lewis and Meg Randa of Sherborn, Emily's owners and caretakers.

The story of Emily the Cow, who escaped from a Hopkinton slaughterhouse, is being made into a movie by "First Look Pictures."

The News will receive its trophy at an award ceremony in April in the Los Angeles Ballroom of the Century Plaza Hotel in Century City, Calif. That show will be taped for broadcast later in the spring as a 90-minute special on the new "Animal Planet," to be followed by an encore presentation on the Discovery Channel.

A number of celebrities have lent their names to the Ark Trust and supported the foundation's efforts, including Beatrice Arthur, Brigitte Bardot, Alec Baldwin, Kim Basinger, Sid Caesar, James Cromwell, Ellen DeGeneres, Dr. Jane Goodall, Mariette Hartley, Tippi Hedren, Earl Holliman, Casey Kasem, Richard Kinley, Jack Lemmon, Rhonda Flemming Mann, Rue McClannahan, Kevin Nealon, Brooke Shields, Alicia Silverstone, Loretta Swit, and Stephanie Zimbalist.

BRIEF LIVES

The true story of a black and white heifer who escaped from a Massachusetts slaughterhouse a year ago is about to be made into a movie. Emily the Cow is getting star treatment, including her own television and video recorder in the barn. Udderly unbelievable? That's Hollywood.

Here is the noos: A year ago, Emily threw her 1600 lbs of choice cuts over a gate out of a Massachusetts slaughterhouse and disappeared into the woods. After 40 days she was rescued by the Randa family, animal-rights campaigners.

Emily, movie star: First Look Pictures has bought the rights to the Emily saga and has begun work on the screenplay. Ellen Little, who heads the company, has paid for the construction of the $10,000 barn and has pledged a lifetime endowment for the cow.

The Cow Appreciation Society: Fans flock to see her. Last winter, she was a bridesmaid at the wedding of a vegetarian couple who vowed in the barn to love, honor, and forsake all steaks.

Herd the Latest? Emily dabbles in politics. " She's spokescow for vegetarianism," says Lewis Randa. "People meet her and never want to eat meat again."

The Next Step: Emily decides she needs a stage name, and calls herself Goldie Horn. She becomes celebrated for her catchphrase, which is "Heifer nice day."

Slash and Churn: Doubtless she will soon outgrow the barn. A hacienda-style mansion in Hollywood Hills beckons.

Even Cowstars get the Blues: Fame and fortune, it seems, are not enough. The Randas give Emily a playmate – a six month old steer named Gabriel.

The Future? Following the success of Babe, a movie about a talking pig, the film roles pour in. After milking her fame for all it's worth in Hoof's Afraid of Virginia Woolf? and Horned to be Wild, Emily gets political and makes They shoot Cows, Don't They? – an allegorically, socially aware response to the BSE crisis and she gives Shakespeare a whirl, winning plaudits for her finely judged Kate in the Taming of the Cow. She also lands a singing contract and breaks into the charts with her version of I Heard it Through the Grapevine

Emily's new barn, full of hay, provided by Elllen and Rob Little of Los Angeles. (Photo by Stephen Tackeff, Middlesex News)

THE COW WHO SAVED HERSELF

By Michael Ryan

Emily knew that danger was near. She had never been in a place like this before -- a little shed with a 5-foot-gate behind her. All of her companions had gone through the swinging doors in front of her, and not one had returned. The men who had locked the gate at Frank Arena's slaughterhouse in Hopkinton, Mass., were now off having lunch. Emily saw her chance, and she took it.

When she made her move, jaws dropped and workers stared in amazement. Suddenly, Emily -- all 1400 pounds of her -- was airborne, sailing over the gate. "A cow just can't do that," Meg Randa told me. As residents of this rural area west of Boston were to discover, Emily, a 3-year-old Holstein, can do many things cows aren't supposed to do.

Frank Arena and his workers took off after their runaway animal, but she disappeared into the woods and eluded them all day. It was November 1995, the beginning of an odyssey that would capture the imagination of the entire community. Slaughterhouse workers scoured the woods, leaving out bales of hay to entice Emily back into their grasp. She would have none of it.

Instead, people reported seeing her running with a herd of deer, learning from them how to forage in the wood. Soon the local paper was running updates on Emily sightings. Meg Randa read the first one. "The wheels started turning," she told me. "I said, 'There's got to be some way we can purchase her and let her live in peace.'"

We were in the former town hall in Sherborn, Mass., near Hopkinton. Meg and her husband, Lewis, bought the building 12 years ago. Here, they run a school for children with special needs. Devoted to Quaker nonviolence, they also operate the Peace Abbey, where seminars and conferences on peace have attracted participants like Mother Teresa and the Dalai Lama. Surely, if they could bring Mother Teresa to a little farm town in New England, they could do something for a desperate cow.

The Randas had hundreds of co-conspirators. Emily sightings suddenly dried up -- it seemed that nobody wanted to see her captured. Local farmers started leaving out bales of hay for her to eat.

Meg called Frank Arena at the slaughterhouse and was touched by his willingness to help. His granddaughter, Angela, had given Emily her name, and even Frank (who died unexpectedly in January) seemed

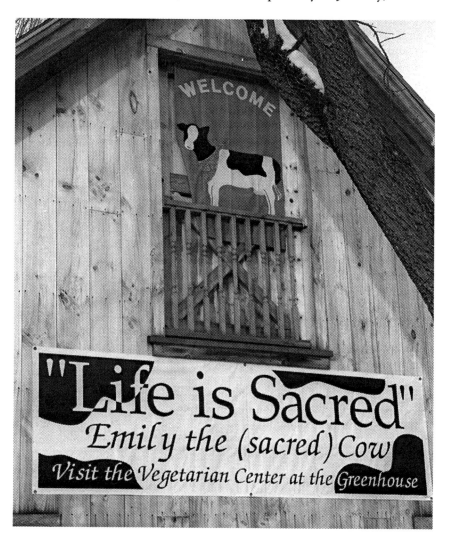

173

Emily's New Sacred Cow Barn (Photo by Lewis Randa)
impressed by her pluck. At first he offered to let the Randas have Emily for the bargain price of $350; then, after consulting his granddaughter, he changed the price to $1. "He liked the idea of Emily being at the school," Lewis Randa explained.

A blizzard hit, and Emily's food sources were covered by snow. The Randas and others brought grain, hay and water to places where they thought Emily might be found; the food was eaten after they left, but Emily wasn't ready to reveal herself.

Finally, one December day after they spread out some food, the Randas saw Emily. "We looked over our shoulder, and she was right there looking at us," Meg recalled. Emily had lost 500 pounds and needed veterinary treatment after her 40-day ordeal, but the loving care of the students at the school has brought her back to her full weight. And now she has company.

Last December, a neighbor approached the Randas and asked if they could take in a calf that might otherwise be sent to a slaughterhouse. The day I visited, little Gabriel stood patiently while Emily groomed and licked him as fastidiously as any loving mom. They have been joined by a pair of turkeys, a mother goat and her two kids, and three rabbits -- all of them rescued from inhumane conditions and all of them now tended by students from the school.

But Emily's biggest test is yet to come. Ellen Little, producer of 1995's film "Richard III" has started work on a film version of Emily's saga. Emily will not have to leave her happy home for the lights of Hollywood, though. She will be played by another Holstein -- and that should give another cow a chance to become a star.

Emily Struggles To Survive Cancer

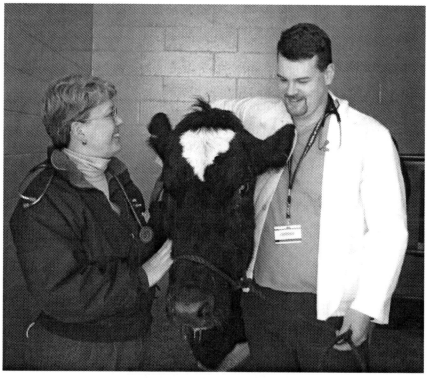

*Emily at Tufts Veterinary Hospital in North Grafton, MA
with Drs. Mary Rose Pradis and Shane DeWitt.*

BOVINE SURVIVOR BATTLES FOR HER LIFE

By Andy Smith

SHERBORN   As incense burned, a Hindu priest chanted and the sun began its dramatic descent yesterday afternoon at the Peace Abbey, Emily the Cow ate bananas and once again fought to escape death.

The 10-year-old cow that drew national attention in 1995 by freeing herself from a Hopkinton slaughterhouse has been diagnosed with bovine leukemia virus.

Emily's caretaker, Meg Randa sensed something was wrong when the cow started acting lazy and withdrawn. Randa also noted changes in Emily's digestion and excretion, so she and her husband Lewis took the cow to Tufts New England Veterinary Hospital in Grafton, where veterinarians discovered cancer in her uterus.

Randa and her family gathered around the cow with friends yesterday for a healing ceremony led by Krishna Bhatta, a priest at Lakshmi Hindu Temple in Ashland. With a gravelly, deliberate voice, Bhatta prayed for Emily while a dozen well-wishers sprinkled rice, powders and flower petals on her.

Focusing his blessings on the cow's stomach, Bhatta lifted the elegant blanket draped over Emily, revealing bare skin that had been shaved during medical procedures. In 1995, after the cow jumped a five-foot fence to escape the slaughterhouse, she wandered through the woods for 40 days. The Randas bought her from the slaughterhouse for $1, tracked her down in 18 inches of snow and brought her to live at the Peace Abbey. Now they must decide what type of medical treatment to pursue for her.

*Krishna Bhatta, Hindu Priest with Sri Lakshmi Temple in
Ashland throws flower pedals on Emily the Cow at The Peace
Abbey in Sherborn Saturday afternoon. Holding the harness is
Meg Randa, Emily's caretaker. (Photo by Ken McGagh)*

Emily could become the first cow to receive chemotherapy. During
the exploratory procedure, veterinarians drained 80 liters of fluid from
her, and more is already accumulating. Doctors say the cow's excess fluid
may help Emily absorb the chemo.

"We need to do some soul-searching and make a decision," Randa
said. "They're hopeful if the chemo is successful, it could add years to
her life. It's never been tried, though, so they really don't know."

Randa is concerned about the treatment's painful side effects. A
veterinarian friend of hers recently suggested homeopathic remedies
that she believes are effective for animals with cancer.

"We're starting to think the holistic route might be the better
option," she said. "It's just getting so beautiful out again, and we want
Emily to enjoy the quality of life she deserves."

Krishna Bhatta, local Priest with the Hindu Temple in Ashland holds a healing ceremony for Emily the Cow in the pasture of The Peace Abbey. Emily has cancer. (Photo by Ken McGagh)

Emily in her stall the night before she died. (Photo by Lewis Randa)

Treatment for cancer in cows is uncharted territory for veterinarians. It's also expensive. Contributions to Emily's bills have been made by several private donors, including Ellen Little.

Little, the president of First Look Pictures, a Los Angeles-based film company, is developing plans for a movie about Emily, which Randa said goes into pre-production this fall. Production plans have been delayed several times in recent years.

All the attention and celebrity status has not gone to Emily's head. She stood patiently throughout the ceremony, displaying what Randa said was "a graceful peace that we all seem to take for granted in these creatures."

At the end of the ceremony, the flowers and blankets were removed from Emily, but a golden string remained. Bhatta wore a similar string on his wrist. Blessing her and praying for her health, he tied the string through a hole in Emily's ear -- the hole left by a tag that once symbolized a fate she must again overcome.

EMILY THE COW'S WARTIME SURRENDER

by Andy Smith

I spent the first Saturday of the war standing ankle-deep in shit. The MetroWest Daily News had asked me to cover a Hindu healing ceremony at the Peace Abbey in a small farm town. The Abbey is a former public library that's been converted into a school, barnyard, and non-denominational place of worship. Over three acres of land rest monuments to Gandhi, Mother Theresa, Martin Luther King, and John Lennon. Every turn is a celebration of pacifism, veganism, environmentalism, etceteraism. It was a difficult week for the Peace Abbey and its directors, the Randa family. They'd led 18 war protesters to a local military research center, where they were arrested for attempting to block the entrance. But the real bad news came the following day when Emily the Cow was diagnosed with uterine cancer.

In 1995, Emily escaped death by jumping the gate of a slaughterhouse and fleeing into the woods. For a biblical 40 days, she roamed the Earth, aided by an underground railroad of sympathizers who intentionally misdirected her would-be captors. When Emily was caught on Day 40, Christmas Eve, she had lost so much weight that she was worthless to the slaughterhouse. The Peace Abbey purchased her for $1 and nursed her back to health. Eight years later, Emily was once again looking death in the eye.

A veterinarian convinced the Randas that chemotherapy could extend Emily's life. She would be the first cow to receive such treatment, but they decided it was worth a shot. Emily the Cow was penciled in for a Wednesday appointment.

But first there would be a healing ceremony, which, as mentioned, took place on the first Saturday of the war in a pasture full of shit. A dozen

*Krishna Bhatta, Hindu Priest rings bell at ground altar
to honor Emily the cow. (Photo by Ken McGagh)*

new-age hippies circled around Emily, still radiating in the afterglow of their civil disobedience arrests. A Hindu priest draped an elegant blanket and scarves over Emily, and chanted quietly while sprinkling her with rice and flower petals. He rubbed ointments on Emily's belly, where it had been shaved during the exploratory procedure that found the cancer. There were incense, jellies, fruits, and lots of concerned facial expressions.

As ridiculous as it all was, I can't remember the last time I felt as peaceful as I did at the Peace Abbey. The priest's words were the only sound in the pasture. It was the closest thing I'd experienced to silence in months.

I'd been having a little trouble sleeping. The "decapitation strike" explosions that started the war got in my head. I heard them relentlessly. I don't know why. I'd seen gruesome depictions of war in movies and T. V., and I'd read about the battlefield's deathly stench. But I'd never thought about how noisy war must be. The sheer volume of a bomb falling in your neighborhood has to be terrifying. In bed I would lay awake, my imagination obsessing over the sound of cruise missiles striking. Even without the bombs, it was already shaping up to be a very noisy war.

Lewis and Meg Randa with Emily as they prepare for the healing ceremony conducted by local Hindu priest. (Photo by Dan Dick)

There were jerky anti-war types shouting their empty slogans, whining about Bush, and brainlessly demanding a utopia that will never exist. Jerky hawks giving condescending reminders that those quaint little dissenters make America what it is. Droning on about "bringing democracy to the region," as if it were as simple as "just add water."

Moron talk-show hosts engaging moron callers chanting, "U-S-A!," and enjoying it all, way too much. Blathering anchors generating an endless stream of overused meaningless words and phrases: "targets of opportunity, embedded reporter, freedom fries, the plan, the dossier, the coalition of the willing, the hearts and minds." I never want to hear these words again. By Day Three, the war had produced more babbling than any war in history. And everyone was certain their babble was the right babble. I was exhausted. Exhausted by the battle in my brain to figure out where I stood. Exhausted by the inescapable noise. But there was nothing to hear out in that pasture.

After 20 minutes of the spiritual nonsense, Emily grew restless. Mrs. Randa tried to keep her stationary for the priest, but Emily seemed intent on wandering. Wandering toward me. As she got closer, I tried to

Emily with Lewis during blessing ceremony. *(Photo by Dan Dick)*

hold my ground without looking frightened or disgusted. But I'd never been so close to a cow in my life. And suddenly this big cow face was no more than five feet from mine. The priest didn't miss a beat, proceeding through his rituals as Emily and I stared each other dead in the eye. She looked pathetic. Snot dripped from her nose and mucus lined her eyes. As I took in her cow breath, I was overcome by a profound and soothing sense of kinship with Emily. She had approached me with such conviction, as if she was seeking me out. Perhaps she understood the absurdity of both our situations. Perhaps she recognized we were both stuck in worlds we'd long since given up trying to understand. Lunatics surrounded us, and circumstances were spinning out of control. The best we could do was survive. But I knew Emily would not. There was death in those eyes. I think she wanted me to know she would soon be escaping the slings and arrows of life. I think she wanted me to know she was going someplace better. And someday I would too.

PEACE ABBEY MOURNS DEATH OF EMILY THE COW

Visiting hours and memorial service will be held next week

SHERBORN   Emily the Cow, who caught the attention of the region and ultimately Hollywood when she escaped from a Hopkinton slaughterhouse eight years ago, has died.

Sherborn's Peace Abbey, where Emily has resided in tranquility since her dash to freedom, announced Emily's death yesterday in an e-mail to the cow's countless supporters

"Please e-mail us with your story on how Emily touched your life. Thanks for taking time to respond in her honor. Our hearts are broken," the Abbey's message states.

The cause of death was uterine cancer. Emily was 10.

A movie about Emily's exploits, detailed in The News eight years ago, is being made into a Hollywood movie. A script is now being finalized, according to the producers.

Emily jumped the gate at the Hopkinton slaughterhouse and escaped into the woods where she remained for 40 days until members of the Peace Abbey caught her and paid $1 to the slaughterhouse to keep her.

A memorial service will be held tonight at 7 PM in the Quaker room in the Abbey Conference Center in Sherborn's historic center (at the junction of routes 16 and 27.)

"Emily was an amazing creature that blessed the lives of thousands and helped countless people on their journey to vegetarianism," the Abbey wrote in their e-mail.

The e-mail ends with an anti-war message: "And with Emily's passing comes a reminder that when human beings wage war, defenseless animals pay the biggest price."

Cal Hottelet, Jayne Hamel with daughter Ali Koehler and Ruthann Grundfast bless Emily's grave site before a small replica of the statue of Emily which was being created. (Photo by Lewis Randa)

EMILY THE COW PASSES AWAY

By Christine Moyer

SHERBORN   Made famous by her miraculous escape from a slaughterhouse in Hopkinton in 1995, Emily the cow passed away on Sunday morning. The 10 year old died in her sleep of uterine cancer.

Adopted at age 2 by Meg and Lewis Randa, co-directors of The Peace Abbey in Sherborn, Emily inspired many who visited her. Emily's amazing story caught the attention of the region and ultimately

*Emily with the golden thread in her ear the day
before she died. (Photo by Lewis Randa)*

Hollywood. "She's more than just a cow. She's a symbol of hope," Lewis Randa said last week.

On a cold November day in 1995, the 1600 pound Holstein heifer bolted from the killing floor of the slaughterhouse, leapt over a 5 foot gate and fled from her captors for 40 days and 40 nights. Originally worth $500, the owner of the slaughterhouse asked Randa to pay only $1 if they could catch Emily.

"We found her hiding in a pine forest," Meg Randa said about Emily, who was taken to the Peace Abbey on Christmas Eve, 1995.

Lewis and Meg run a spiritual retreat center and a school for special needs children and young adults. Since her adoption, Emily enjoyed life at the Peace Abbey, serving as a motivational figure for many people across the country.

Meg Randa said, "many in the Hindu community think she is a messenger to the world to be compassionate."

To others, Emily is a role model. Lewis Randa described a woman's struggle to leave an abusive relationship, which was resolved after visiting Emily at the Abbey.

Originally, the Randas were considering using Tufts University's innovative chemotherapy treatment on Emily. However, they finally chose to let her life end as it began – naturally.

"We'd rather she be at the Peace Abbey to die," said Meg Randa.

A memorial service was held on Tuesday.

QUIET ACTIVIST EMILY THE COW WILL REST AT THE PEACE ABBEY

Famed bovine fled slaughter, inspired vegans

By Benjamin Gedan, Globe Correspondent

SHERBORN   Eight years after escaping a Hopkinton slaughterhouse, Emily the Cow, a soft spoken, but persuasive spokeswoman for vegetarianism, died in her sleep early Sunday of uterine cancer. She was 10.

Officials at the Sherborn Peace Abbey, which saved Emily in 1995, praised her yesterday for promoting vegetarianism to the center's estimated 100 weekly visitors. In her eight years in Sherborn, hundreds of visitors forswore red meat, many taking the vegetarian pledge after encountering the mild-mannered activist, said Meg Randa, who runs the Peace Abbey with her husband, Lewis.

"She changed the way people think about animals," Randa said yesterday. "It used to be easy to go the meat counter at the grocery store, then Emily put a face on that package of beef."

The Peace Abbey, a rural complex for contemplation and anti-war activism in Sherborn's historic district, also houses the Greater Boston Vegetarian Resource Center. Its 3-acre property, with three buildings, is splattered with anti-war posters, many critical of the conflict in Iraq.

Vegetarianism, however, is also part of the pacifist mission, officials said, and pamphlets including "Veg News," "Veg Living," and "Why Vegan?" are stacked throughout the grounds.

The center offers cooking classes and discussion groups to promote vegetarianism, and officials said Emily the Cow was central to the regional campaign.

Emily lies in a state of holiness in the barn during her
two day wake. (Photo by Lewis Randa)

"A lot of people were touched by her," said Lewis Randa.

Emily joined the Peace Abbey's herbivorous campaign at age 2, after a celebrated escape from a Hopkinton slaughterhouse, and weeks of wandering through snow-covered woods. Aided by an "underground railroad" of animal lovers, the cow eluded capture for 40 days, before the Peace Abbey was allowed to buy her for $1 thanks to Frank Arena, owner of the slaughterhouse.

"[Emily] was the poster child for vegetarianism," said Christine Cassidy, a Lesley University student and Peace Abbey intern. "She was very popular. Jumping from the slaughterhouse to freedom was quite a story."

Yesterday, mourners trickled into the Peace Abbey barn, where the black-and-white cow lay motionless, her 1,300-pound frame shrouded in a colorful, embroidered blanket, a floral necklace around her bowed head.

Lewis Randa digs Emily's grave behind statue of Mahatma Gandhi at the Pacifist Memorial. (Photo by Meg Randa)

Emily's death was not unexpected; the cow was diagnosed with cancer in February, and last Tuesday, she returned from the Tufts University Hospital for Large Animals with painkillers, her owners having opted against experimental surgery and chemotherapy.

Longtime companions, however, were shaken yesterday as funeral preparations were underway. Including the sizable corpse, signs of Emily's death were ubiquitous. A despondent recording on the Peace Abbey answering machine, and a sandwich board in its driveway, reported Emily's demise. A tractor and forklift for moving the body were parked next to the barn. And bright orange cones were arranged in the grassy yard, marking a cemetery plot in the shadow of a Mahatma Gandhi statue.

Testimonials will be heard tonight at a memorial service at 7. The cow's life will be permanently recalled in a life-size bronze statue to be erected above the grave, which workers planned to dig with the tractor's backhoe. "It's a shame that her life was cut short. Her work was not

*GRAVE BLESSING: Conrad and Mandy Gees, Joe Font
and Dan Dick recite peace prayers at Emily's open grave.
(Photo by Lewis Randa during short ceremony)*

done," said Meg Randa, who reported a doubling of Peace Abbey traffic
since the start of the war in Iraq. "She was an extraordinary creature,"
added Lewis Randa, holding back tears. "When she was living, she was
a sight to behold."

EMILY HOOFS IT TO COW HEAVEN

Peace Abbey resident succumbs to cancer after escaping slaughter

by Peter Reuell

SHERBORN   As spokeswomen go, Emily was never really all that talkative.

But all it took was one look in her wide, brown eyes and the occasional "moo," and most folks at least contemplated putting down their cheeseburger for good.

Dozens of friends and fans of the Holstein with heart, turned out at the Peace Abbey in Sherborn yesterday to say goodbye to the cow who became a national *cause celebre* and poster animal for vegetarianism.

"It's amazing we're all here because of a cow," Peace Abbey co-director, Meg Randa, marveled. "She was just extraordinary. I feel like her job wasn't done ... but I know her legacy will continue if we carry her in our hearts."

The boisterous bovine first captured the region's attention eight years ago when she jumped a gate at the Hopkinton slaughterhouse and fled into the nearby woods.

Aided by supporters opposed to the eating of meat, Emily managed to stay on the lam for 40 days before members of the Peace Abbey finally cornered her and negotiated a $1 fee with the slaughterhouse to keep her.

Since then, Emily led a life of ease in the lap of heifer luxury – sleeping in the warm barn with all the hay she could eat.

Earlier this year, however, tragedy came calling.

*Philip and Pam Boulding of Magical Strings perform at the
Memorial Service for Emily the Cow in the Quaker Room at the
Peace Abbey Conference Center. (Photo by Meg Randa)*

In February, Emily was diagnosed with uterine cancer, and within
weeks, officials at the Abbey decided against having her undergo an
experimental regimen of surgery and chemotherapy.

The 10 year old cow was found dead in her stall Sunday.

"Emily was an amazing creature that blessed the lives of thousands
and helped countless people on their journey to vegetarianism," Abbey
members wrote in a message posted on the Center's Web site.

Many who attended the memorial for Emily remembered her as an
animal with an uncanny ability to touch people's lives.

The brave bovine's tale even reached all the way to Hollywood.

A film version of the Emily story has been in the works for years,
but Ellen Little, President of First Look Pictures, yesterday said they
hope to begin pre-production within the next year.

We hope the film will be part of her legacy," said Little after learning
of Emily's death. "She has affected already so many people's lives, and
we hope this will continue with the film. I'm sorry it didn't happen in
her lifetime."

PAYING RESPECTS TO EMILY THE COW

By Carol Beggy & Al Young, Globe Staff 4/2/2003

STOPPING TO SAY GOODBYE   A steady stream of visitors stopped by the Sherborn Peace Abbey yesterday to pay their respects to Emily the Cow, who died Sunday of uterine cancer. After escaping from a Hopkinton slaughterhouse eight years ago, the 10-year-old cow made headlines worldwide and was regarded as a prominent symbol of vegetarianism. Last night, Emily was remembered at a memorial service in the Quaker room at the Peace Abbey.

"It's actually been quite beautiful - all the outpouring of support we've received ... e-mails from all over the world," said Lewis Randa, who, along with his wife, Meg, runs the Peace Abbey, a complex for contemplation and antiwar activism that houses the Greater Boston Vegetarian Resource Center.

Emily will be buried at the Peace Abbey, not far from a statue of Gandhi and from the barn where she lived for her last eight years. The story of Emily's escape and her life in a custom-made barn in the suburbs is being chronicled in a feature film.

IN AMERICA: ZEN OF EMILY

By Miryam Wiley

Emily the cow died last weekend, but her spirit lives. She was a source of inspiration to this mother of a child with special needs. The same way the bigger challenges come from the outside world rather than everyday life at home, truly meaningful content arises from listening to a repetitive sentence that seemed meaningless at first.

It took me a while to tune in to Emily, the cow who jumped over a fence and escaped the slaughterhouse eight years ago. After weeks of hiding in the woods of Hopkinton, she was taken in (and paid for) by Lewis and Meg Randa of the Peace Abbey in Sherborn.

For one year now -- ever since my daughter Katherine started attending the Life Experience School of the Peace Abbey -- news of people and animals alike became the norm in our conversations.

Emily provided entertainment and love, a presence that left everyone around in a cheerful mood. Recently, however, the news had turned to sadness.

"Emily is sick," Katherine told us one day. And then we learned Emily would possibly get chemotherapy, a choice eventually dropped to avoid the difficult side effects.

Still, Emily did not leave our thoughts. At breakfast and dinner, we often heard of visits to the Abbey and interactions with the famous cow or the news of how difficult things were for her.

Then, last Sunday, Emily died. And to my surprise, I was left with deep sadness.

The first day it was just sad news. Then it sank in and it got worse when Katherine let out a deep cry one night.

I feel like I've lost Emily the same way I felt when I lost Mr. Rogers a few weeks ago. Like him, Emily was a barometer of all things good.

The special kids at my daughter's school understood, in their own way, that Emily lived to prove a point. Emily was symbolic of a struggling creature that had a lot of dignity to pass on to others. Near her, many made a quiet and caring choice.

"People came to meet Emily and were amazed to find that she was extremely interested in them," said Meg Randa. "She was very affectionate and displayed the same kind of personality and intelligence as, perhaps, their dog. One would never consider eating their dog so, perhaps, the connection was made that eating an animal was no longer acceptable to them."

If all people didn't become vegetarians because of Emily, they knew they had in her a good reason to consider it. I have been there and back long before Emily was around. I succumbed to a carnivorous lifestyle while eating on the road as a TV reporter in Brazil. But I know the bounty of nature and I feel I must reconsider.

For this whole past year, whenever we met new people and Katherine was asked the name of the school she attended, she often said, beyond

Emily with Meg (Photo by Lewis Randa)

the name: "The place where the famous cow lives. Don't you know about Emily the cow?"

I saw more than one person look pretty terrified of being uniformed.

The conversations started to flow when others saw Katherine had no trouble with this topic, and details about how the cow escaped the slaughterhouse and what a special cow this was!

As inattentive as I might have been, I now know better than to dismiss the importance of Emily.

In conversations with pacifist Lewis Randa about the state of the world in recent weeks, Emily seemed to be part of the talk here and there. Even, one time: "The Metrowest Daily News loves Emily!" he said.

Looking at the book of Emily clippings that goes back to 1995, I can see this paper did, in fact, give Emily a lot of press time, despite some critics who didn't spare the readers their view of the ridiculous "moo-vement."

In my house, the spirit of Emily lives. And despite the fact that I was not one who paid her a visit or got one of her famous cowlicks, I have realized I must tune in.

"Emily was more than just a cow," said Lewis Randa. "She was, for people who loved her, an important creature who put them in touch with a greater understanding of animals and how humans should treat them. Her eyes would melt your heart and make you appreciate what animals have to offer."

I think she was so inclusive that she made a difference in humans' appreciation of each other as well.

"We must learn that animals are thinking, feeling creatures with the same will to live that any other creature possesses," said Meg Randa. "She was an ambassador for all animals, and her life is testimony to the fact that all life is sacred."

IN AMERICA: 'O COME ALL YE FAITHFUL TO UNWRAP EMILY

By Miryam Wiley

Meg Randa remembers a day at the Peace Abbey in Sherborn when an 18-month-old baby was lost and the mom was panicking. Everyone was moved when the baby was found inside the fence with Emily the cow, who was licking the baby's head right by her feet. Of course the cow could have stepped on the baby, but she didn't. "Emily was always alert and aware, always careful around people," says Randa.

Emily is the cow who jumped over a 5-foot fence, escaped the slaughterhouse and after weeks wondering around Hopkinton, was eventually bought by the Randas, the leaders of the Peace Abbey, and brought to live there. Over the years she proved to be more than a cow and became a symbol of compassion.

Now, on Dec. 24, even if some of us are worn out and overspent in more ways than one, there is chance of renewal at a ceremony to honor Emily the Cow on the grounds of the Peace Abbey.

The event is scheduled at noon Christmas Eve day. A bronze statue to honor the cow that lived there for eight years will be unveiled on what will be called the Sacred Cow Animals Rights Memorial.

Emily's statue was created by Lado Goudjabidze, from Long Island City, N.Y., the same artist who sculpted both the Gandhi and the Mother Teresa statues at the Abbey. The new statue will be delivered from the foundry on Dec. 20. This date commemorates the ninth anniversary of the very day the Randas read about her in the paper and decided it was their call to adopt her.

Christmas Eve was the night the Randas were actually able to persuade her to trust them and get into a trailer that brought her home.

201

Sacred Cow Animal Rights Memorial before bronze statue
of Emily the Cow arrives. (Photo by Lewis Randa)

"We see it as a form of synchronicity," said Meg Randa. "With all the commercialism and the hubbub about Christmas, what a wonderful way to unwrap this beautiful Christmas present. It feels to us that Emily is coming back to us on Christmas Eve."

Lewis and Meg Randa made the news when they decided to adopt the cow that escaped the slaughterhouse. Now they seem ready to take the world's reaction to their latest gesture to include Emily once again.

"To most people it probably seems absurd that we are bringing a statue of a cow to the Peace Abbey, but Emily had a very deep connection with people," said Meg Randa. "She looked you in the eye and changed you. It is hard to put it into words."

For Lewis Randa, Emily's significance is one of a saint.

"Erecting a statue of a cow surely seems strange if you didn't know Emily, but not all that odd if you understand the significance of the Sacred Cow in the East," he said. "In the West, it is customary to see statues of saints at Abbeys. We at the Peace Abbey know something about Emily that others don't, but soon will. The animal kingdom, to no one's surprise, produces saints too -- that is, if we don't kill and eat them first."

The statue of Emily will be 6 feet tall and 8 feet long. Placed over Emily's grave on the grounds of the Peace Abbey, this memorial will match the style of the existing Pacifist Memorial, with many quotes of note from famous vegetarians, such as Henry David Thoreau: "I have no doubt that it is part of the destiny of the human race, in its gradual improvement, to leave off eating animals."

And Albert Einstein: "Nothing will benefit human health and increase chances for survival of life on Earth as much as the evolution to a vegetarian diet."

Meg Randa said that at the ceremony they will tell the story of how Emily escaped the slaughterhouse, then spent 40 days and 40 nights walking around with the deer until she was found.

"This bovine serves to remind us that all life is sacred, and that all animals hold greater value to the world than being a source of food," said Lewis. "Emily's life story challenges us to include the rest of God's creatures in the circle of compassion."

Emily's distinction won't end at this. Her life story will also be the subject of a film to be done in Canada. But for now, it's in real life that she will be remembered and celebrated, not only for what she brought to people, but to encourage political views and attitudes toward the whole world.

Lewis said, "if Mother Teresa traveled from India to visit the Abbey in '88, it seems strangely appropriate that a few years later Emily would come along. She and Mother Teresa were highly evolved beings from two different species from the same part of the world. The Sacred Cow Memorial will bless people who visit in ways beyond anything they could imagine."

EMILY STATUE DELAYED BUT NOT FORGOTTEN

By Jon Brodkin

SHERBORN   The Peace Abbey wanted to cancel yesterday's Christmas Eve tribute to Emily the Cow. The $98,000 statue of what some consider a "sacred" bovine wasn't ready for its unveiling and so people at the Abbey figured it was better to wait. But when Peace Abbey founder and director Lewis Randa started calling people involved in the ceremony to tell them it was off, they insisted that it go on without the statue, he said.

"We did our best to cancel this but couldn't," Randa told a group of more than 50 Emily lovers gathered at her gravesite for a noontime ceremony.

Nine years ago, Emily escaped a slaughterhouse in Hopkinton by jumping a five-foot gate, and then evaded capture for 40 days before being bought by Randa and his wife, Meg, for $1. For many, she became a symbol of and reason to practice vegetarianism.

She died of uterine cancer in March of last year. The next month, some of her hair and blood were taken to the Ganges River in India, where cows are considered sacred.

The Peace Abbey, a multifaith center that also has statues of Gandhi and Mother Teresa, expected to unveil a six-by-eight-foot bronze statue of the cow yesterday, the ninth anniversary of the day Emily arrived at the Peace Abbey.

The statue was expected to arrive two weeks ago, but was held up by a delay at a foundry in Newburgh, New York.

"We were saddened to learn the statue would not be here," Lewis Randa said, expressing hope it will arrive before Valentine's Day.

Some Peace Abbey members chose to view the delay as only fitting, given Emily's success in avoiding capture when she was a young cow on the lam.

"It's just like the Emily story," said Ernie Karhu.

"She'll be found when she wants to be found," Marylyn Rands asserted.

Emily's grave, where yesterday's ceremony was held, is named the Sacred Cow Animal Rights Memorial. A plaque on the gravestone says, in English and Hindi, "Wars kill animals too."

During the ceremony, water from the Ganges was sprinkled onto Emily's grave, a prayer and song for Emily were recited, and the cow's admirers related stories about her.

Meg Randa said she first knew they had a "sacred" cow when the trailer with Emily pulled into the Peace Abbey.

"She kind of threw her head out of the trailer and locked eyes with the Gandhi statue," Randa said.

From the beginning, Emily's story struck a nerve with people. After she escaped the slaughterhouse, people in Hopkinton helped her on her way, in part by leaving hay bales out for her to eat, Randa said.

"She managed to touch the hearts of people in Hopkinton," she said. "They supported her by forming what we came to know as an underground railroad that kept her safe."

Emily was described as a friendly, people-oriented cow, and was credited with helping a young man who broke his hip while doing chores at the Peace Abbey. Corty Woods, a member of the Abbey was taking care of the animals about two years ago when he slipped on some ice. "No one could hear his calls for help, except for Emily, who began bellowing so loudly that someone came out to help Corty," Meg Randa said.

"He kept saying 'Emily saved my life,'" Randa said "She really was extraordinary in that way."

PEACE ABBEY HONORS
ITS SACRED COW

By Ray Hainer

SHERBORN   At noon on Christmas Eve, while many folks were traveling or shopping frantically for last-minute gifts, dozens of people flocked to the Peace Abbey for a look at a bronze cow. That is, they came to see the unveiling of a large bronze statue of Emily the cow, a longtime resident of the Peace Abbey considered a sacred animal, a symbol for vegetarianism and a cherished pet by many at the multifaith retreat center.

The unveiling never occurred -- the foundry in Newburgh, N.Y., that is casting the statue is behind schedule -- but a spirited tribute to the cow was held anyway. Emily, who died of cancer last March, became a minor celebrity of sorts nine years ago, when she escaped from a Hopkinton slaughterhouse and survived in the surrounding woods for 40 days and 40 nights.

Lewis and Meg Randa, the directors of the Peace Abbey, bought Emily from the slaughterhouse for $1 after seeing news reports of her escape, and brought her to the Peace Abbey on Christmas Eve 1995. Although Lewis Randa said the Peace Abbey was deeply disappointed to learn that the statue was not ready, its absence did not seem to diminish anyone's enthusiasm for the event. In fact, as one member of the Peace Abbey pointed out, the late arrival of the statue was only fitting for a cow who played by her own rules. "It's like Emily is embodied in the statue," said Ernie Karhu. "It was always in her nature to be elusive. She'll come in her own time."

Unfazed by the delay -- or the frigid weather -- a group of 60 people crowded onto a circular brick-and-granite path known as the Sacred Cow Animal Rights Memorial. Adults with camcorders and young children in colorful jackets and scarves huddled together on the memorial, located just a few yards from a memorial to pacifism which features a larger-than-life-size bronze statue of Gandhi. At the center of the Animal Rights Memorial is a large granite slab that marks Emily's grave and will eventually serve as the base for her bronze likeness.

On Friday, the slab was draped for the occasion in a sacred blanket from India that Emily used to wear, and was also dotted by several photos and other small ornaments. A small metal censer sat on the ground nearby, steadily emitting puffs of aromatic smoke. The ceremony was a casual, free-form affair: memories of Emily were shared, mottoes from plaques that adorn the Animal Rights Memorial were read aloud ("Cow protectionism is Hinduism's gift to the world," "Wars kill animals, too"), and a prayer written specially for the occasion by Dot Walsh was recited. Meg Randa recalled the moment, nine years ago to the day, when she and her husband first brought Emily to the Peace Abbey.

Yogendra Jain, a follower of Jainism, an Indian faith which holds that all living things have a soul, led the gathering in a prayer for peace. Afterwards, he used a small silver bowl and pestle to sprinkle water from the Ganges River over Emily's grave, a small bronze replica of the statue and the heads of the crowd.

And on a different note, Ali Koehler, a student at the Peace Abbey's Strawberry Fields school, sang "Emily," a wistful song from the film "The Americanization of Emily," a 1964 comedy set during World War II starring James Garner and Julie Andrews. Throughout the wide variety of tributes, the impact Emily had on those who knew her was evident, as was her importance to the Peace Abbey.

"Emily, never having given birth, bonded with people the way she would have bonded with her offspring," Lewis Randa said at one point. "We were blessed to be her offspring, in a certain sense."

The ceremony may well have heightened the anticipation for the statue among those who attended, but they are not likely to be disappointed when it finally does arrive. The statue, which has a price tag of nearly $100,000, will stand 6 feet tall and will measure 8 feet from nose to tail. "It will just take your breath away," Meg Randa told the crowd Friday. "It's the second-best thing to having Emily here."

The Randas said that they hope the statue will be delivered by the end of January. They are considering holding an unveiling sometime around Valentine's Day.

73

EVEN AFTER DEATH, EMILY STILL ELUSIVE

By Ben Montgomery

ROCK TAVERN   Men are working everywhere. Men in white suits that look like grown-up pajamas. Men in masks and bandannas. Men with grinders, with saws and sanders; men with pencils planted behind their ears; men in the process of creating.

In the middle of this gigantic factory beside Route 17K, in the middle of all these men, is a cow named Emily who is late for a party. Way late. Twenty-two days late. She should have been there Christmas Eve.

Sixty people at The Peace Abbey in Sherborn, Mass., were waiting for her in the cold, with jackets and camcorders, near a bronze statue of Gandhi, in a special place called the Scared Cow Animal Rights Memorial. Why isn't Emily here? the children wondered. Hold that thought.

NINE YEARS AGO, in November of 1995, Emily the cow was packed in a stinky shed with her herd at a slaughterhouse in Hopkinton, Mass. She watched as her companions disappeared through a set of doors in front of her, never to return. If cows can contemplate, Emily must have figured it out: She was next. Ahead was death by bovine butcher. Sirloin. Hamburger. Chopped liver. Someone's meal. Behind was freedom – in the form of a 5-foot gate. Emily chose the latter.

According to newspaper accounts of the escape, the 1,600-pound Holstein sailed over the gate and disappeared into the woods, udders flopping, stunned men scrambling to catch up. In the days that followed, Emily became a legend. The slaughterhouse staff tried to entice the 2-

year-old heifer back into her fate with bales of hay. No dice. Folks across the rural community west of Boston would report Emily sightings to the local press. She was seen here, then there, then foraging in the forest with a herd of deer. But soon the sightings dried up. Seemed folks wanted Emily to make it out there in the world.

Word spread like stink at a feedlot. A group of hippies caught wind and called the guy who owned the slaughterhouse. Impressed by the whole deal, the fella offered to sell Emily to the hippies for a buck. After 40 days and 40 nights on the biblically timed lam, Emily revealed herself to Meg Randa, a vegan, activist Quaker who runs a beautiful, harmonious place called The Peace Abbey with her husband, Lewis. They got Emily a barn with amenities like a TV and VCR. She lived in heifer happiness

People magazine covered Emily's story. So did Parade and a few TV stations. Someone wrote a children's book, someone bought rights to the moo-vie. Then Emily died. Last March. Cancer. The folks at The Peace

Lado Goudjabidze examines bronze casting of Emily the Cow which was delayed in foundry in upstate New York. (Photo by Lewis Randa)

Abbey couldn't just let her go, so they commissioned a bronze life-sized statue of Emily – reportedly for around $100,000. She would stand in the Sacred Cow Animal Rights Memorial, near the statue of Gandhi, between plaques that read "Cow protectionism is Hinduism's gift to the world" and "Wars kill animals, too." Sculptor Lado Goudjabidze was commissioned to create Emily in clay. Metallurgist Dick Polich would handle the rest. She would be unveiled at a ceremony on Christmas Eve, marking the day in 1995 when Emily was brought to The Peace Abbey.

Christmas Eve came and went. Emily was a no-show. The folks at The Peace Abbey sort of expected that. "It's like Emily is embodied in the statue," Ernie Karhu told the Dover-Sherborn Press. "It was always in her nature to be elusive. She'll come in her own time."

On a cold day in January, 185 miles away in Rock Tavern, N.Y., a bronze Emily still stood in Dick Polich's foundry. Something stalled on the artists' end, says Chris McGrath of Polich Art Works. "But," she says, "we're not going to point fingers." Either way, the cow is nearly finished. Maybe by the end of the month. "We're close," Polich says. "We still have to attach the birds and some flowers." A set of lights on a stand shine down on Emily in the middle of this huge building, in the middle of all these men working to get her finished. Her eyes are bronze, untarnished, and she looks like she has seen things.

She looks like she'll move when she wants to.

SACRED COW COMES HOME

By Carol Beggy & Mark Shanahan

COW COMES HOME, AGAIN   Early Friday evening Meg and Lewis Randa, who run the Peace Abbey in Sherborn, arrived at the center with a life-size statue of Emily the Cow, who escaped a Hopkinton slaughterhouse and lived out her days in a custom-built barn promoting a message of nonviolence and vegetarianism. Emily was bought by the Abbey in 1995, and until her death two years ago, she drew thousands of visitors (hundreds of whom forswore eating meat) and attracted media attention from around the world. The statue was made at a foundry in Newburgh, N.Y., and a crane was on site to place the statue on Emily's grave on the property, which also has a larger than life-size statue of Gandhi.

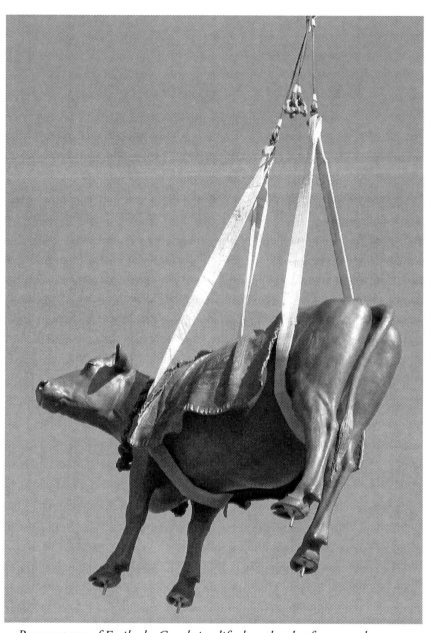

Bronze statue of Emily the Cow being lifted on the plateform over her grave at the Sacred Cow Animal Rights Memorial. (Photo by Lewis Randa)

PEACE ABBEY HONORING ITS SACRED COW

By Jennifer Rosinski, Globe Correspondent

SHERBORN   A crowd of people. Eloquent speeches. A bronze memorial statue. It sounds like a familiar scene. But this weekend in Sherborn, something will be different. The honoree will be a cow.

A statue of Emily the Cow, who became a national sensation after her escape from a Hopkinton slaughterhouse 10 years ago, will be dedicated at the place where she once found sanctuary.

"Emily is part of a much larger message," said Dot Walsh, program coordinator at the Peace Abbey. "If we want to save the earth, we need to pay attention to the vegetarian lifestyle, because growing cattle harm the earth."

"Cows are fed grain and lots of it. It takes 12 pounds of grain to produce one pound of meat," said Lewis Randa, cofounder of the Abbey. "In a world where people are starving to death, the meat-centered diet needs to be challenged."

The 3 p.m. ceremony Sunday in front of the statue coincides with an annual Vegan Potluck lunch held by the Boston Vegetarian Society at the Abbey.

Speeches proclaiming Emily's status as a symbol of nonviolence and vegetarianism will be given by Peace Abbey founders Lewis and Meg Randa, Krishna Bhatta of Ashland's Sri Lakshmi Hindu Temple, and guest speaker Camilo Mejia, a Florida National Guardsman who was imprisoned for a year after refusing to return to his unit in Iraq following a two-week leave in 2003. The Peace Abbey is a pacifist retreat and education center founded in 1988. The Abbey houses a

213

Life-size bronze statue of Emily the Cow being hoisted by a crane on to the granite stone above her grave. (Photo by Erin Prawoko, Metrowest Daily News)

pacifist memorial and museum, national conscientious objector registry, a chapel, and a vegetarian resource center.

Emily's statue, designed by sculptor Lado Goudjabidze, sits atop her grave in what the Abbey calls The Sacred Cow Animal Rights Memorial. A statue of Indian independence leader Mohandas K. Gandhi, which Goudjabidze also created, sits nearby. "Lado has given [Emily] a life past her physical life. If you look into her eyes, there is compassion and a connection to her," Walsh said of the cow statue, which has already drawn hundreds of visitors. "It's deeply moving." Emily died on March 30, 2004, less than a month after she was diagnosed with bovine leukemia. She was buried at the Peace Abbey in April. Her statue arrived one year later. Emily's saga began Nov. 14, 1995. The 1,500-pound cow was lined up in front of the A. Arena & Sons slaughterhouse in Hopkinton, waiting her turn to be chopped into steak. But Emily had a different idea. The two-year-old Holstein leaped over a five-foot-high gate and ran into the woods while workers were on a lunch break. Her escape -- and her 40-day run for freedom -- caught the attention of the world's news media. The Randas captured the cow, and a jittery and skinny Emily ended up at the Abbey that Christmas Eve after the Randas paid the slaughterhouse $1 for her.

PEACE ABBEY WELCOMES BRONZE STATUE OF EMILY, ITS BELOVED BOVINE

By Maureen Sullivan

SHERBORN Nearly 10 years after she avoided becoming somebody's dinner, and more than a year after she died, Emily the cow has returned to town. This time in bronze. Weighing in at 2,300 pounds, about 800 more than she did in real life, a statue of the beloved bovine arrived at the Peace Abbey Friday afternoon in an open U-Haul, with Lewis and Meg Randa towing and the sculptor, Lado Goudjabidze, driving right behind them all the way from the foundry in Newburgh, N.Y., 3 1/2 hours away." It's so wonderful. We've been giddy since 5:30 this morning, (when they went to New York)," said Meg Randa. "I was watching Emily in the rear-view mirror the whole time. It's wonderful to have Emily come home. You can feel her spirit here."

The statue was supposed to have arrived in December, then earlier this year, but, Lewis Randa said, "Guess she was meant to be unveiled on Earth Day. What better time to honor Emily and her message?" The statue's new home is over the grave marker of the real Emily, who died of cancer in the spring of 2003. The site is surrounded by tablets set in stone that extol the virtues of nonviolence and a vegetarian lifestyle.

There is also a larger tablet that gives a summary of Emily's life at the Abbey, from escaping a local slaughterhouse in late 1995, to her becoming a symbol of vegetarianism and nonviolence.

Emily is located behind the statue of Gandhi that also was sculpted by Goudjabidze. There were two short ceremonies marking the statue's arrival. The first took place while Emily was still in the truck, waiting to be unveiled and moved by a crane. After a few words of thanks from

Lewis and others, including Goudjabidze and Paul Carey of Strata Bank, which provided the financial backing for the statue, the head and body were uncovered to an appreciative audience of about 30.

"Lado got Emily's eyes just right and captured her spirit," said Meg Randa.

Dot Walsh, the Peace Abbey chaplain, also noticed the eyes. She said that while she was visiting the artist's studio in New York City, she told the sculptor that the eyes weren't right. The sculptor ended up working another 50 hours on the head and eyes and everyone now agrees the statue depicts Emily and her spirit perfectly. In addition to that detail, Emily the statue wears a blanket, a garland of flowers and has a hole in her left ear. According to Meg Randa, the blanket is a replica of one given to Emily by a visiting group of Hindus (the original is at the Peace Abbey); the flowers are another Hindu sign of respect; and the hole is from Emily's pre-Abbey days when she was supposed to be slaughtered. It's where she wore her ID tag.

In her final days, the hole was decorated with a gold thread, part of a healing ceremony conducted by a Hindu priest from the temple in Ashland. Once unveiled, Emily was strapped up again and became airborne. She was moved about 80 feet in the air, then about 100 feet over to the gravesite, where a granite slab was waiting with pre-drilled holes. Once the statue was in place, Lewis Randa gave the face a loving and gentle touch, then had a golden thread placed in the ear. Walsh led the others in a short prayer before Lewis Randa wrapped it up with a "Viva Emily!" An official dedication is slated for Father's Day.

SHERBORN HAS SACRED COW

By Lindsey Anton

SHERBORN   A Father's Day ceremony fit for royalty honored one of Sherborn's own: Emily the Cow.
The bronze statue of the bovine at her Peace Abbey grave was officially dedicated Sunday as the Sacred Cow Animal Rights Memorial. People filled the grounds to pay respect to the cow who gained international attention after escaping a Hopkinton slaughterhouse 10 years ago.

Quaker elder and pacifist Elise Boulding of Needham watches as the 2,300 hundred pound statue of Emily the Cow is placed at the center of the Sacred Cow Animal Rights Memorial. To the left is Audrey Bourque of Bellingham. (Photo by Erin Prawoko, Metrowest Daily News)

Shake and Lado Goudjabidze, sculptors from New York City stand with Meg and Lewis Randa admiring the statue of Emily the Cow following the dedication ceremony on Earth Day.

The statue, created by Lado Goudjabidze, looks like an average bovine, but Emily stands for much more.

Emily's story is one of survival, perseverance and inspiration. After hearing of Emily's escape, Meg and Lewis Randa, Peace Abbey co-founders, brought her to live at the Peace Abbey. After eight years in town, Emily died March 30, 2003, of cancer. A statue adorned with a blanket and flowers, Hindu signs of respect, stands at her eternal resting place, where Emily the Cow will live on as a symbol of vegetarianism, animal rights and nonviolence.

The dedication turnout showed that Emily was a beloved bovine, accepting of all who visited. Krishna Bhatta of Ashland's Sri Lakshmi Temple and Viren Shah, Jain Center of Greater Boston president, blessed the sacred statue with flowers and water from the Ganges River in India.

Cherish life

The Randas, Evelyn Kimber, President of the Boston Vegetarian Society and Camilo Mejia, a Florida National Guardsman who spent a year in prison after refusing to return to what he considered an illegal war in Iraq, remembered Emily. Hundreds came to spread her message: cherish life.

Meg Randa said Emily attracted more visitors to the Peace Abbey than anyone else ever has and "there was something about this cow." Randa said guests would meet Emily and foreswear meat.

"Just meeting Emily changed so many hearts," she said.

Dot Walsh, the Peace Abbey chaplain, said Emily helped her to be more compassionate, kind and loving. Walsh was touched by these selfless traits that people came to observe in Emily. She welcomed people without preference for anyone in particular.

Mejia, recognized by Amnesty International as a prisoner of conscience, thanked Emily for the "invaluable message of peace and justice she left for all of us."

As a vegetarian, Mejia believes his diet leads to a nonviolent lifestyle, and he said people "must reject the principle of violence."

Carrie Haigh, of Milton, never met Emily, but after hearing the kind words at the dedication, she wishes she had. She believes Emily represents peace and nonviolence.

Haigh, a Peace Abbey supporter, said Mejia's stance against war brought her to the ceremony. Haigh said there's a relationship between Emily and Mejia, and she supports "the whole notion of peace to all creatures."

Harold Brown, farm sanctuary outreach coordinator, urged this concept at the ceremony and stressed the importance of a cruelty-free world, starting with animals. He said making friends with animals can help people have compassion for others.

"It's so important that we all reach out," Brown said.

And that's what Emily encouraged people to do. Whether it's a change in diet or lifestyle, the Sacred Cow Animal Rights Memorial reminds people that they can make a difference.

"There's no telling how many people this memorial will touch," Lewis Randa said.

EMILY THE COW
A Legacy of Non-Violent Living

By Kathleen O'Brien

A statue honoring "Emily the Cow" was dedicated this past weekend at the Peace Abbey, in Sherborn. Emily gained fame by escaping from a slaughterhouse and eventually finding a home at the Abbey. People who were within earshot of the Peace Abbey in Sherborn this past Sunday might have thought it strange to hear the sound of Barbara Streisand singing "Emily, Emily, Emily…" but the crowd attending the service just beyond the Gandhi Pacifist Memorial thought it entirely appropriate. Emily the cow was a sacred animal; touching the lives of many by teaching them about peace, non-violence, and compassion for all living things. In a community where the front building is dedicated to Martin Luther King, Jr. and Bobby Kennedy and the Peace Abbey itself is dedicated to Mother Teresa, a life-size, bronze memorial over the resting place of Emily is just as significant. Emily came to the Peace Abbey's Veganpeace Sanctuary on December 24, 1995 after being on the lam for forty days following her escape from a slaughterhouse in Hopkinton. "There was something about Emily that defied description," said Lewis Randa, director of the Abbey, and certainly the people who came to support Emily shared that sentiment.

The Abbey community, believing in ethical vegetarianism, shared this dedication with members of the Shri Lakshmi Hindu Temple of Ashland. Cows are sacred animals in the Hindu faith, and the statue was given a special blessing by two priests from the temple. Also present were representatives of the Jain Center of Greater Boston and the Boston Vegetarian Society. A member of the Jain Center sprinkled water taken

Photo sent in by unidentified friends of Emily. Emily knew them well. She had lots of friends who came and went, maintaining a connection with Emily that was deep and abiding and in many cases lead to a life long commitment to a vegetarian life style.

from the Holy River Ganges in the City of Benares, India. The same priest from Shri Lakshmi who blessed Emily's statue, had previously placed on her a sacred cow blanket, flowers, and put a golden thread through the hole in her ear (where her slaughterhouse nametag had once been) when she was diagnosed with bovine cancer.

At the time of Emily's passing, friends of the Peace Abbey who were traveling in India released clippings of her hair, traces of her blood, and the golden thread into the Ganges River. Harold Brown, from the Farm Sanctuary in upstate New York, also spoke about his involvement with vegetarianism and with Emily. Brown, ironically, a former beef farmer, stated that animals are individuals and to truly find peace, one must cross the species barrier by extending kindness to animals. Through this act of compassion there is hope for extending it to all people. Brown concluded, "animals are always in the present moment and experience life from the heart." Dot Walsh of the Peace Abbey spoke about the four virtues she learned from Emily, compassion, courage, kindness, and love. Emily, who loved bagels, Wonder bread,

Krishna Bhatta, Hindu Priest with Sri Lakshmi Temple in Ashland blesses statue of Emily the Cow at The Peace Abbey in Sherborn Saturday afternoon. (Photo by Lewis Randa)

and especially children, inspired many people to extend their efforts in non-violent living through vegetarianism and veganism.

The statue itself, with deep and engaging eyes, truly evokes a human spirit through Emily's image. Surrounded by plaques with quotations about animal rights, both in English and Hindi, the statue carries a message which extends beyond Emily's life; the right to life for all living things is holy, an emotion echoed by speaker Camilo Mejia. Mejia, an Amnesty International "prisoner of conscience" and the first conscientious objector to the Iraq War, was court marshaled and then imprisoned for his beliefs. Mejia spoke about Emily as "a fugitive of senseless violence." He was supported, by all the people in attendance, in his belief that killing is unnecessary and only fuels corporate greed. Mejia explained that his vegetarianism began while in the service as a way for a more healthy existence, but quickly it became an issue of morality. Mejia spoke about the essentiality for the respect of life and how Emily so beautifully illustrated this point while asking for nothing in return.

Close up of statue of Emily the Cow with flowers and golden thread in ear. (Photo by Lewis Randa)

The observance concluded with everyone reciting the Twelve Prayers for Peace, which are from the twelve major religions of the world and displayed on plaques at the Pacifist Memorial. In a tribute to Emily, a plaque beneath her feet asks people to consider refraining from eating meat for the rest of the day, or the rest of their lives.

Surrounded by people who continue to love and cherish the memory of Emily, her legacy is simple in its approach towards love and kindness. In the company of words that serve to strengthen the meaning of Emily's life, one plaque in particular speaks to the humanity of vegetarian lifestyle. These are the words of Alice Walker, writer, activist, and feminist, who said, "The animals of the world exist for their own reasons. They were not made for humans any more than black people were made for white, or women created for men."

HOLY COW

By Elizabeth Eidlitz

Only a nursery-rhyme cow could jump over the moon, and only an extraordinary bovine could vault a locked five-foot holding gate to escape from a slaughterhouse in Hopkinton, Massachusetts. But on November 14, 1995, Emily, a two year old, three-quarter-ton Holstein, who "just said no" to becoming someone's sirloin steak dinner, eluded her captors and disappeared into the woods.

*Animal rights activists Mary and Matt Kelly visit
Emily's grave. (Photo by Meg Randa)*

Boston Vegetarian Society President, Evelyn Kimber with noted author and activist Howard Lyman at the annual BVS gathering at Emily's Memorial. (Photo by Lewis Randa)

The escapee captured the rural community's imagination: residents, forming an ad hoc underground railroad, shielded her whereabouts from police and slaughterhouse employees, pointing them in the wrong direction of sightings. Local farmers left out bales of hay while Emily was learning to forage with a companionable herd of deer. Students and staff at The Peace Abbey in Sherborn, Massachusetts, established by Quaker activists Lewis and Meg Randa as part of a learning center for special needs children, joined local conspirators.

When blizzards covered the ground, the Randas and others left grain, hay, and water at places where they thought Emily might be found. After forty days and forty nights in the Massachusetts wilderness, where she'd lost five hundred pounds and run off much of her commercial value, Emily revealed herself on Christmas Eve. "We looked over our shoulder, and she was right there looking at us," says Meg, who coaxed the heifer into a trailer with a bucket of feed. The A. Arena and Sons slaughterhouse finally sold Emily to the Randas for one dollar.

Abbey member Bram de Veer speaks at memorial ceremony about how he and his wife Elizabeth organized and assisted the Temple priest in the traditional sacred cow ritual on the Ganges River in India in April 2003 honoring Emily. (Photo by Meg Randa)

The Randas ate their Christmas dinner with Emily in the Abbey barn, where many animals rescued from inhumane conditions have found sanctuary: Gloria, a Holstein who burst off a truck and soaked two adopted veal calves with kisses; a pair of turkeys, Thanks and Giving; a goat, Belle, with her two kids, Jacob and Joshua; a Yorkshire sow, Babe, and the next to last of her litter of nine, Henry VIII.

For eight years, Emily, who served as bovine-of-honor at several weddings that took place in the Abbey barn, catalyzed a new awareness in people by her presence. She died of uterine cancer in March 2003. A month later, a Hindu priest in India, assisted by Abbey members Bram and Elizabeth DeVeer, released hair clippings from Emily's forehead and from the tip of her tail, traces of her blood, and a piece of golden thread, which had been placed through the ID tag hole in her ear, into the holy river Ganges.

Emily was buried at The Peace Abbey in April near statues of Mother Teresa and Gandhi. Over her grave is a life-sized bronze likeness weighing twenty-three hundred pounds. The $100,000 statue wearing a blanket and a garland of flowers was designed by Lado Goudjabidze, an internationally acclaimed artist and sculptor from former Soviet Georgia, and is the centerpiece of the Sacred Cow Animal Rights Memorial, which was dedicated at a Father's Day ceremony in June 2005.

80

MY THOUGHTS ON EMILY

By Kathy Berghorn

Emily, thank you for the gift of your presence in my life. It was, quite simply, your gift of presence that I will remember most about you. You were always purely and simply present, always in the moment. You invited every person who came to you to do the same.

During my many visits to you in your barn over the years you lived at the Peace Abbey, I now realize that I was receiving darshan. You reminded me of the true meaning of the word darshan, which simply means "sight" in Sanskrit -- sight of a sacred being.

When I think of the many elaborate efforts I had made over the years before meeting you to receive darshan at the feet of human spiritual teachers, I can only smile. I have waited in line for hours for a momentary hug from Ammachi and have driven to another state to hear Mother Theresa address an audience of thousands. Certainly these great beings had their own special gifts to share but how different was your darshan in its utter simplicity! The door to your barn was always open. Often there were other visitors there to see you and often we were alone. There was no protocol to being with you, no schedule of events. You were open and accessible to all. There were no boundaries of culture or religion. The apparent difference of species didn't seem to matter either.

You were a living reminder that we are all One. You made no distinctions and reminded us to do the same. You catalyzed a new awareness in people by your very presence. One look into your large, luminous brown eyes communicated so much more than words ever could. Who can say how many people felt a new awareness of compassion as they stood quietly with you? I've heard you whimsically described as the "poster girl" for vegetarianism but you lived beyond all "-isms" and you changed people not by rhetoric or reproach but simply by your being. You gave wordless testimony to the urgent necessity for an all embracing compassion. You embodied the title of Michaelle Small Wright's book " Behaving As If the God in All Life Mattered." Speaking humbly and gratefully for myself, this is your legacy to me personally, Emily. I must recommit to living as if the divine presence in each and every being matters. This will be a lifelong journey and not an easy one in a world where not all beings live in the state of all-inclusive harmlessness that you did.

Your memory will be an ongoing reminder that it is important to try. I will continue to fail often, to be sure. The memorial to be erected in bronze and marble in your memory will be an outward and tangible sign of your continued presence in the heart of every person whose life you touched and the countless lives you will continue to touch after the passing of your physical form. I feel very blessed to have known you in that physical form and will always be grateful for the joy you brought to my life and the lives of all the family members and friends I brought to see you. "Let's go see Emily!" we would say, and a happy sense of anticipation always filled us as we pulled in through the gates of the Peace Abbey and made our way over to the barn.

Our visit this Sunday followed the usual pattern until another visitor told us of your passing. Emily, I wish I had known you were sick. I would have come and given you Reiki. I wish I had known your body was lying in the barn draped in sacredness and surrounded by flowers so that I could have come and been in your peace-full presence one last time. I wish I had known about your memorial service so I could have been present. I realize, however that these regrets are all about me and not about you.

There can be no "final respects" to you, Emily, and there can be no closure until the last slaughterhouse has closed its doors, until all beings show compassion to each other, locally and globally. This is a process that will outlive me, too. Your courageous life journey will be an ongoing reminder that I must never give up. You never did.

Kathy Berghorn

Emily at side of barn, (Photo by Meg Randa)

81

TAKEN FROM
CHAPEL PRAYER BOOK
AT THE PEACE ABBEY

April 4, 2003

Emily, I did not know you. You were in the hospital
when I visited the Abbey for the first time.

Today I felt your presence in Lewis remembering you. I saw and
touched and smelled your blanket from India and I visited your grave.
I will return to the Abbey with children; one will be named Emily.

In the mean time and forever, may God bless abundantly everyone
who knew you and learns of you in the future and bless all whom
they know and will know until this blessing includes everyone
who has lived, is living or will be living in the entire world.

Namaste,

Cecilia Gilchrest

82

"Emily Means I Love You."

Connie Lawson, during Emily's memorial service.

Buddhist Nuns from Nepal staying at The Peace Abbey visit Emily before leaving to work on a sand mandala at Wellesley College. (Photo by David Morey)

Dot Walsh blessing statue of Emily the Cow while reciting the Emily Prayer which she authored. The prayer is cast in bronze in both English and Hindi. (Photo by Lewis Randa)

THE EMILY PRAYER

Dearest Emily, Patron Mother of all Animals
both living and deceased:

We ask that you help and guide us as we walk through life
following your gentle and compassionate example.

For those who struggle with a vegetarian lifestyle, give
them the courage to take one day at a time, remembering
your courage in escaping the slaughterhouse.

For those who seek to follow the path of nonviolence,
help them to see all beings as their brothers and
sisters, in the circle of love, just as you did.

For all of us, Emily, continue to help heal the suffering and wounds
not only that we inflict, but also those that are inflicted upon us.

And in our final hour, help us to pass on in peace, knowing
that our lives have made a difference in this world.

A gift of prayer in gratitude from Dot Walsh,

Abbey Chaplain

Appendix

An animal rights publication in 1985 polled its readers about their religious beliefs. The majority had none. About 65 percent considered themselves agnostics or atheists, placing themselves dramatically at odds with most Americans - 90 percent of whom believe in God. Further, a later academic study concluded that church attendance increases in inverse proportion to belief in "rights" for nonhuman animals (ibid). That is - the more a person goes to church, the less likely she believes animals ought not be eaten, worn or tested upon. Animal rights, an emphatically secular movement, has little to do with theology. And theology has little to do with animals. Both, we believe, are impoverished by these deficiencies.

Theology traditionally has focused primarily on the relationship between humans and God, and the wondrous dance between them.

This has made a certain amount of sense.

Humans are rightly concerned about the human condition, and consciously contemplating God may be of interest to our species alone. But our species may very well not be God's interest alone.

And if the animals do matter, then God have mercy on us, because we are torturing and killing billions of them every year.

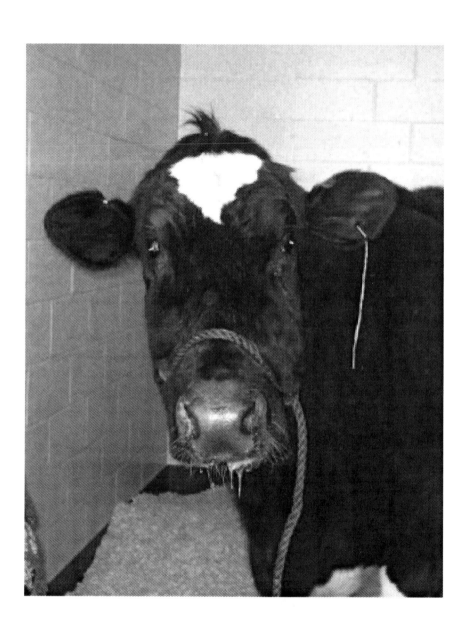

This theological analysis was written before Emily's passing in 2003.

WIDENING THE CIRCLE OF COMPASSION: *INCLUDING EMILY IN OUR THEOLOGICAL VISION*

Introduction

By deciding to tell the story of Emily the Cow, and to understand her story theologically, we undertook a curious task. Many theological analyses with moral undertones begin with implicit shared assumptions, needing no explanation or exploration. For example, if we were to analyze a news story in which children were tied to looms and forced to work 16-hour days, we would all begin with a shared assumption that such treatment was wrong and seek to find theological meaning in the matter. Likewise, if we were to launch an analysis of the United States political scene before women were granted the right to vote, we would begin with the assumption that women ought to have the same rights to citizenship as men.

Here, in this project, there is no such assumption.

The three authors of this project do share a common conviction that animals matter, are significant in God's creation, and ought not be treated and killed as they are. This conviction is a minority opinion. Therefore, we sought here to first make explicit our conviction, argue, and defend it, illumine why it is difficult to hold this opinion in the face of mainstream theology, and then conduct an analysis. This meant undertaking an ambitious project. However, it is one that we hope will be helpful to the theologically minded, the friends of animals, and, mostly, somehow, to the animals themselves.

Respectfully and in peace,

Mary Margaret Earl
Trevor S. Maloney
Susan Roman

THE STORY OF EMILY THE COW

"The love for all living creatures is the most noble attribute of man."
Charles Darwin

As fantastic as it sounds, this story is true. It is not a fairy-tale, and it is not from children's storybook. In November of 1995, it was business as usual at the A. Arena & Sons slaughterhouse in Hopkinton, Massachusetts. The cows were lined up to go through the large swinging doors onto the killing floor to be slaughtered, and then cut up for steaks, hamburgers, and all the other things humans produce from cows. Then, during the workers' lunch break, all this changed. It seemed that at least one cow sensed that danger was near.

Emily the Cow had just seen several other cows go through those doors and not return. In a desperate attempt, Emily ran towards the five-foot high gate, and with a mighty leap heaved her 1,500-pound body over the top. The workers stared in amazement as the escapee ran off into the woods. After picking up their jaws from the floor, the men chased after her to bring her back to the slaughterhouse. Emily, as the cow came to be known, was too wily for them, though, eluding A. Arena and his sons for forty days and forty nights as she wandered in the wilderness.

The locals of Hopkinton, a small, rural town started rooting for Emily. The local paper started running "Emily Sightings" (she was often seen foraging with a herd of deer). Farmers started to leave out bales of hay for her. Arena & Sons continued searching, with the help of the local police, determined to catch her and finish the job. They didn't count on popular resistance, though; the people of Hopkinton gave the police and slaughterhouse employees faulty information, sending them on a wild-cow chase through the woods. Odd, considering that most of these people were, and still are meat-eaters.

Right outside Hopkinton, Meg and Lewis Randa, devout pacifists, run Strawberry Fields, a school for children with special needs, and the Peace Abbey, an animal sanctuary and conference center that has attracted Mother Teresa of Calcutta and honored the Dalai Lama at a Harvard Conference. The Randas, committed vegans, were struck by the plight of Emily, and decided to do something about it. Meg contacted the slaughterhouse and offered to buy the cow. Frank Arena offered to sell the cow for $500, and then lowered his price to $350, as Emily had lost a lot of weight during her time in the forest. After consulting his three-year old granddaughter, who named the cow Emily, she was sold to the Randas for the bargain price of $1. "[Frank] liked the idea of Emily being at the school," explained Lewis.

Disaster struck! A blizzard hit Hopkinton, covering Emily's food in 18 inches of snow. The Randas and their students set out food and water for Emily. When they returned, the food and water would be gone, but Emily was never spotted. "All I could think of was Emily out there in the snow," said Meg (People). Finally, one day in December, after leaving out some food, Emily was spotted by the students and staff of Strawberry Fields. The Randas approached Emily carefully, reassured her that they do not eat animals, and coaxed her into a trailer with a bucket of feed and a lot of pushing. Emily had lost over 500 pounds and needed veterinary treatment, but soon enough she was back to full weight, living safe from Arena & Sons, and enjoying the attention of the students at Strawberry Fields and the media.

Since Emily's daring escape and rescue, Emily has been the focus of attention at Peace Abbey. Producer Ellen Little of First Look Pictures, Hollywood, bought the film rights to Emily's story for a sum that will provide Emily with food, veterinary care, housing, and companionship for the rest of her life. Little also donated $10,000 for a new barn and an attached educational center focusing on vegetarianism and animal issues. A group of Hindu priests from India stopped at the Peace Abbey to visit Emily, believing her to be the reincarnation of a sacred cow. (www.meat.org/cow_escapes.htm)

Today, Emily still lives high on the hay at The Peace Abbey, sometimes receiving letters from fans telling how her story influenced them to stop eating animals. As Meg Randa says, Emily is an ambassador of compassion for animals.

What Has Theology To Do With Animals?

"We have enslaved the rest of animal creation, and have treated our distant cousins in fur and feathers so badly that beyond a doubt, if they were to formulate a religion, they would depict the Devil in human form." -William Ralph Inge

An animal rights publication in 1985 polled its readers about their religious beliefs. The majority had none. About 65 percent considered themselves agnostics or atheists, placing themselves dramatically at odds with most Americans - 90 percent of whom believe in God (Lowe 41). Further, a later academic study concluded that church attendance increases in inverse proportion to belief in "rights" for nonhuman animals (ibid). That is -- the more a person goes to church, the less likely she believes animals ought not be eaten, worn or tested upon. Animal rights, an emphatically secular movement, has little to do with theology. And theology has little to do with animals. Both, we believe, are impoverished by these deficiencies. Here, we want to specifically address the latter.

Why ought we spend our time considering a cow like Emily? After all, there is an abundance of human suffering and joy eminently worthy of our consideration. Millions of men and women are dying of AIDS in Africa. Children in Iraq starve. People with physical disabilities overcome great odds to achieve great things. The world throbs with human drama. Why, then, consider a cow?

We believe Emily's story speaks to a profound truth in the world, and on this we stake our theological claim: God cares about all living creatures, and all these creatures -- men and women and cows and eagles and chickens and dolphins -- are connected. Emily's life, and her escape, matter in the world. And the joy with which humans greeted her freedom, though they eat and wear cows just like her, speaks to that not-yet-severed connection we feel in the best part of our humanity. And that is worth our theological consideration.

Theology traditionally has focused primarily on the relationship between humans and God, and the wondrous dance between them. This has made a certain amount of sense. Humans are rightly concerned about the human condition, and consciously contemplating God may be of interest to our species alone. But our species may very well not be God's interest alone. And if the animals do matter, then God have mercy on us, because we are torturing and killing billions of them every year.

Once upon a time, it may not have mattered so urgently for theology to bother with the animals. Perhaps the animals, many of them, got by all right on small family farms and in an abundance of wilderness. This is less and less often the case in the Western world. Jim Mason in Animal Factories writes: Farms like the ones of my childhood are rapidly being replaced by animal factories. Animals are reared in huge buildings, crowded in cages stacked up like so many shipping crates. On the factory farm there are no pastures, no streams, no seasons, not even day and night. Animal-wise herdsmen and milkmaids have been replaced by automated feeders, computers, closed-circuit television, and vacuum pumps. Health and productivity come not from frolics in sunny meadows but from syringes and additive-laced feed. (xiii)

These are the animals slaughtered yearly in the U.S: More than 37 million cattle; 110 million pigs; 4 million horses, sheep and goats; 8 billion chickens and turkeys (Eisnitz 61). Eric Marcus in Vegan: The New Ethics of Eating, however, puts the total figure at somewhat less -- closer to 8 billion (149). The numbers are so big they seem irrelevant, like trying to comprehend the national deficit. Marcus quotes animal advocate Gene Bauston, who rescues sick and abused animals from slaughterhouses: "It's easy to say eight billion ... but it's impossible to grasp the enormity of the suffering. Eight billion means one animal raised under harsh conditions and then slaughtered, then a second animal, then a third animal, and on and on until you reach eight billion" (149). Emily was nearly one such animal.

Theology and philosophy have defined human beings over and against these animals. The conclusion, explicitly or implicitly, is that humans matter ultimately to God, while the animals don't. The reasons are reasons of consciousness or language or some other special category in which only humans supposedly belong (and once upon a time, only some humans belonged). This distinction between humans and animals has enabled us to treat animals grievously. Joy Williams in her Harper's essay "The Inhumanity of the Animal People" writes: St. Francis once converted a wolf to reason. The wolf of Gubbio promised to stop terrorizing an Italian town; he made pledges and assurances and pacts, and he kept his part of the bargain. But St. Francis only performed this miracle once, and as miracles go, it didn't seem to capture the public's fancy. Humans don't want to enter a pact with the animals. They don't want animals to reason. It would be an unnerving experience. It would bring about all manner of awkwardness and guilt. It would make our treatment of them seem, well, unreasonable. The fact that animals are voiceless is a relief to us, it frees us from feeling much empathy or sorrow. If animals did have voices, if they could speak with the tongues of angels -- at the very least with the tongues of angels - it is unlikely they could save themselves from mankind. Their mysterious otherness has not saved them, nor their beautiful songs and coats and skins and shells, nor have their strengths, their swiftness, the beauty of their flight .... Anything that is animal, that is not us, can be slaughtered as a pest or sucked dry as a memento or reduced to a trophy or eaten, eaten, eaten (pg. 60).

Theology, in an effort to tend to human needs, likewise largely has refused this pact with the animals. We suggest now is the time that theologians are called urgently to the task of redeeming our relationship to the animals.

The Urgency of the Question

The conclusions of religion and theology orient our society's ethical bearings. How we treat women, children, people from another religious tradition, the earth, flow at least in part from our theology. So, too, theology has informed our treatment of the animals. This treatment in the year 2001 has reached horrific proportions. The situation can wait no longer. Theologians must speak to the fact of mass factory farms and slaughterhouses. We must stress here that while we theologically consider Emily's life in specific in this paper, we are not commenting on the conditions of the farm from which Emily came, or the slaughterhouse from which she escaped. We have no knowledge of the conditions of those particular places; they may have been far superior to those that we describe. Rather, we consider here general trends in American farming and slaughterhouse practice. These trends do not fit the images many people hold of farming.

The Modern Factory Farm

Like many aspects of Western culture, farming has become a corporate activity, with large "factory farms" swallowing small family farms and falling under the spell of technology. Animal Factories authors Jim Mason and Peter Singer, for example, point out that between 1955 and 1977, the number of chickens in a single "egg factory" house rose to 80,000 from 20,000 - with the chickens increasingly being squashed together in cages. About 45 percent of birds in 1967 lived in cages in egg-laying operations. Mason writes, "today, 95 percent or more of all egg production comes from caged birds in automated factory buildings" (3). These factories are supplied by "multiplier" companies which allow birds to breed egg-producing chickens. Here are the fluffy chicks we admire at Easter. Half are killed soon after they peek at the world through cracked shells. Mason writes, "males don't lay eggs, and the flesh of these strains [egg-laying chickens] is of poor quality. So they are, literally, thrown away. We watched at one hatchery as "chick-pullers" weeded males from each tray and dropped them into heavy-duty plastic bags. Our guide explained: 'We put them in a bag and let them suffocate. A mink farmer picks them up and feeds them to his mink.' More dismal are the lives of male calves born to dairy cows. They live in the harshest confinement systems" (Mason 12). Taken from their mothers when they are just a day old, they are placed in tiny stalls so they can't move around and toughen their muscles -- so as to make them more desirable as "veal." They are fed milk replacer and made anemic, bred to be more appealing to connoisseurs. Mason visited a veal factory and described what he saw: At feeding time the lights were turned on as the producer made his rounds. In two rooms, more than a hundred calves were crated in wooden stalls. Their eyes followed our movements; some appeared jittery, others lethargic. Many tried to stretch toward us from their stalls in an attempt to suckle a finger, a hand, or part of our clothing. The farmer explained: "They want their mothers, I guess." (Mason 12-13).

Female calves are raised to give milk. Such cows are increasingly kept in "some type of confinement systems" -- Mason estimates about half the 10 million dairy cows are kept thus (Mason 11). The dairy industry has become consolidated, which, Marcus writes, "has put America's milk supply increasingly in the hands of large corporations and has degraded the everyday care of the dairy cow." Cows can live up to 20 years naturally, but they begin producing less milk after five years -- so they are replaced with younger cows (Marcus 125). The older cows are sent, as Emily was, to the slaughterhouse.

The Modern Slaughterhouse

Though the images of factory farm are wrenching, descriptions of the modern slaughterhouse can be especially disturbing -- bringing immediacy to the way we understand the violence animals face in an increasingly industrialized system. Slaughterhouses have become bigger and faster. Twenty years ago, 75 percent of all cattle were killed in 50 companies and 103 individual plants. Five years ago, 40 percent of all cattle were killed by just three firms in 11 plants (Eisnitz, quoting the USDA 62). Humane investigator Gail A. Eisnitz in the 1990s began to look into the treatment of animals in the modern, fast-paced slaughterhouse. Though she considered herself to have "thick skin," she was horrified at what she learned: cows skinned alive, their legs cut off while alive, or beaten with chains, shovels and boards; pigs tortured and beaten and scalded. One problem was that in an effort to be more efficient and "productive" slaughterhouse lines were speeded up, and workers couldn't keep pace - so cows rather than being knocked unconscious immediately, continued down the line still conscious (28-29). Eisnitz wrote about the humans who worked in these slaughterhouses, who were brutalized themselves by being forced to brutalize animals. Eisnitz interviewed a slaughterhouse worker:

One time I took my knife -- it's sharp enough -- and I sliced off the end of a hog's nose, just like a piece of bologna. The hog went crazy for a few seconds. Then it sat there looking kind of stupid. So I took a handful of salt brine and ground it into his nose. Now that hog really went nuts, pushing it nose all over the place .... It's not anything I should be proud of .... It happened. It was my way of taking out the frustration. Another time, there was a live hog in the pit. It hadn't done anything wrong, wasn't even running around in the pit. It was just alive. I took a three-foot chunk of pipe ... and I literally beat that hog to death .... It was like I started hitting the hog and I couldn't stop. And when I finally did stop, I'd expended all this energy and frustration, and I'm thinking what in God's sweet name did I do? (93-94).

Eisnitz' sensitivity to both animals and the human workers showed how humans suffer when they become deadened to their connection with animals. Workers shared stories of drinking to numb themselves, or treating their families badly, or becoming generally violent. One worker said "Every sticker [a job on the slaughterhouse line] I know carries a gun, and every one of them would shoot you ... Most stickers have problems with alcohol. They have to drink, they have no other way of dealing with killing live, kicking animals all day long. If you stop and think about it, you're killing several thousand beings a day" (88).

What was especially difficult for Eisnitz was her inability to get media attention. Major networks considered the subject too gruesome, or they wanted to focus on those aspects that impacted consumers - such as beef contamination (157). In a world that has decided animals are "ours" to do with as we please, it is taboo to ask humans to face the consequences of that decision. Yet, there is no real way of separating the fate of the animals, or of the earth, from the fate of humans. Our fates are intertwined; peace for one relies upon peace for the many. Religion and theology have roles in healing the world's brokenness in many ways -- including reconsidering the worth of the animals like Emily.

Animal Consciousness – Why Did Emily Run?

"The question is not, Can they reason? Nor, Can they talk? But, Can they suffer?" – Jeremy Bentham. Can we attribute to Emily an awareness of impending danger and a ratiocinated escape? If we demur, citing unwarranted anthropomorphizing, can we reasonably posit a state of suffering in the slaughterhouse which Emily would experience and from which she would want to escape? Ordinary common sense would prompt an affirmative answer from many, but science has traditionally and until the 1980's disavowed our ability to talk meaningfully about animal consciousness and animal pain. Bernard E. Rollin, in The Unheeded Cry: Animal Consciousness, Animal Pain and Science[ii], a comprehensive survey and analysis of the subject of animal consciousness, assails the traditionally predominant attitude of animal psychology, zoology and ethology that "animal mentation is unknowable and concern with it is unscientific and scientifically impossible"[iii]. His central premise is that the 'common sense' of science, rooted in positivism and behaviorism, with a correlative rejection of value questions, have precluded the treatment of subjective states of pain and suffering as scientific knowledge knowable from physiology and behavior. This ideology paradoxically repudiates the legitimacy of scientifically discussing animal pain while at the same time animal pain is presupposed in research that attempts to extrapolate human states from laboratory induced animal states.

Happily, Rollin reports that at last the denial of pain in animals is becoming scientifically incoherent. The Cartesian model of animal pain as a mechanical process lacking an experiential and morally relevant aspect is ironically being undone by the increasing discoveries of identical neurophysiological mechanisms in humans and animals, making it highly implausible that animals are automata, if humans are not. Pain and pleasure centers have been found in the brains of birds, mammals and fish and the neural mechanisms regulating pain response, including biofeedback mechanisms for controlling pain, are similar in all vertebrates. Science is finding the neurophysiological correlates in animals for all rudimentary forms of mentation. Of particular relevance to Emily's pre-slaughter state of mind, research indicates that all vertebrates have receptor sites for benzodiazepine suggesting that all have the physiological basis for experiencing anxiety. Denial of pain consciousness is implausible from an evolutionary perspective as well; the subjective experience of pain and the motivations engendered thereby appear no less essential to the survival of animal species than to homo sapiens.

Rollin argues strenuously and persuasively against positivism's demand that only what can be directly observed or experienced is worthy of being deemed factual and that, consequently, states of mentation in animals cannot be established. The positivist statement about scientific legitimacy is a "value judgement, a statement about what ought to count in science, a statement growing out of a particular metaphysics and epistemology, not out of simple data-gathering."[iv] Such a position is not only a metaphysical and valuational choice, it precludes much inter-subjective data which science presumes (e.g. 'public objects') and also ignores the fact that mentation, particularly the attribution of mentation to other humans generally, is one of the categories by which we process reality. We irrepressibly characterize emotive behavior as expressive of underlying mental states. The attribution of mental states, especially those connected to pain and pleasure, leads to the possibility of morality. In the human species, moral concern for others is grounded in the presumption of feeling coupled with some theory of moral imperative.

While ordinary common sense and language have assumed mentation in animals, most conspicuously in human efforts to train and control animals, common sense has consistently ignored the moral problems that issue from attributing thought and feeling to animals.[v] Thus, though common sense might take exception to science's denial of consciousness to animals, it was complicit with science's avoidance of moral concern since scientific, as well as agricultural and other, uses of animals are seen as beneficial to humans. Rollin notes that most popular reactions to the conditions in slaughterhouses and packing plants are "aesthetic revulsion" rather than "moral indignation".[vi]

Rollin charts the rise of social concern about the morality of animal use and its impact on science. In the 1980's, animal pain and its control became a focus in veterinary and laboratory sciences and research began to seriously consider the subjective experience of pain and other noxious emotions in animals. Research is confirming that the attribution of mental states to animals best explains their behavior. Illustrative of this principle and relevant to Emily is recent research regarding stress. It was demonstrated that although the physical stressors applied to a group of animals were identical, variation in psychological stimuli creating varying emotional-cognitive states or attitudes led to radically different physiological signs of stress (as measured by secretion levels of a certain steroid).[vii]

In Rollin's view, the major factor encouraging animal consciousness studies in science has been social concern with farm animal welfare, particularly in Britain. Historically, social concern over animal welfare did not focus especially on farm animals because the traditional agricultural setting was viewed as idyllic, where animals roamed freely in natural settings. As traditional agriculture changed dramatically to intensive methods with animals in extreme confinement managed and manipulated by machinery, the public's "Old MacDonald's Farm" conception had not correspondingly adjusted. An expose published in Britain resulted in the formation of a commission to meet the resulting public outcry and demand to know whether farm animals were suffering.

A substantial scientific effort was then spawned in which common sensical notions and locutions concerning a full range of negative subjective experiences in animals were inserted into an acceptable scientific framework, exemplified in the work of Marion Dawkins.[viii] Dawkins' work gave scientific legitimacy to 'selective' or 'critical anthropomorphism' enabling scientists to reappropriate common sense assertions that animals can experience a broad range of noxious experiences.

The work of Dawkins and others have catalyzed new research into the suffering of farm animals and have led to the introduction of palliative measures. To Dawkins criteria, however, Rollin would add the animal's telos. By this he means, for example "that if an animal has bones and muscles and is given no opportunity to use them, this provides a prima facie reason to postulate suffering".[ix]

The Unheeded Cry inspires us to let our common sense have sway. Then, yes, Emily felt anxious about entering the slaughterhouse. The cause? Perhaps the smell of slaughter, the apprehension of the unknown, the felt collective apprehension of the others around her. It does not require an anthropomorphic leap from this anxious state to the arousal of her 'fight or flight response.' Her escape saved her from the far more heinous suffering of actual slaughter. And, yes, these human-like actions elicited human sympathy. But those humans, and others, must come to regard Emily's actions as intrinsically bovine, the exercise of her natural impulse to fulfill her telos.

A Critique: Anthropocentric Theology and Philosophy (or: Where are the Animals?)

"True human goodness, in all its purity and freedom, can come the fore only when its recipient has no power. Mankind's true moral test (which lies deeply buried from view) consists of its attitude toward those who are at its mercy; animals. And in this respect mankind has suffered a fundamental debacle, a debacle so fundamental that all others stem from it." Milan Kundera

Trying to analyze Emily's story through mainstream theology is -- at best -- like analyzing why leprechauns revel in gold. There isn't much to go on. At worst, the analysis might describe how a machine jumped a fence and denied humans their God-given right to slaughter her. In preparing a sympathetic analysis of Emily's story, we first explore why such an endeavor is a challenge, critiquing the relevant theology and philosophies of St. Thomas of Aquinas, Rene Descartes, Karl Rahner and Paul Tillich. While none of these influential thinkers easily offers their systems to animal-friendly interpretation, we shall see they vary greatly in how much space they leave to consider Emily and others like her. We will explore why such an endeavor is a challenge, critiquing the relevant theology and philosophy.

Aquinas and the Thomistic Tradition

St. Thomas Aquinas is the progenitor of the historically persistent view, still vibrant in the Catholic tradition, that animals were created by God for the service and use of humanity and have no rights whatsoever against humanity. In his Summa Theologica Aquinas raises and answers the question of whether it is unlawful to kill any living thing. The commandment 'Thou shall not kill', wrote Aquinas, is not to be taken as referring to "irrational animals, because they have no fellowship with us."[x] In his Summa Contra Gentiles, he writes that by divine providence the natural order of things is such that the "imperfect" is made for the "perfect". Animals are "intended for man's use in the natural order. Hence, it is not wrong for man to make use of them, either by killing them or in any other way whatsoever."[xi] For Aquinas, animals are not even inherently deserving of any charity, for charity is a kind of fellowship that in his view cannot even metaphorically be extended to 'dumb' animals. Even God loves the animal only in so far as they are of use to humanity.

The Thomist doctrine became the dominant Western theological position on animals unchallenged until the eighteenth century. The notion that the mental superiority of humans legitimates absolute dominion over animals seems rooted in Western consciousness and was perpetuated by Descartes.

Descartes

Peter Singer, in his landmark work Animal Liberation, writes of Descartes' view of animals saying, "The last, most bizarre, and -- for the animals -- most painful outcome of Christian doctrines emerged... in the philosophy of Rene Descartes" (Singer 207). For Descartes, Emily's condition simply would not be an issue. His view of animals totally abdicates man from any responsibility towards the animal kingdom. If humans today actually believed what Descartes believed about animals, then there would be no ground for the occasional animal abuse trials that pop up in our court systems. Descartes did not believe that animals have the capacity to suffer.

For Descartes, there are two principles that cause motion in the human body. The first is the corporeal principle. This principle is purely mechanical, dependent on the construction of organs. Reflexes fall under the corporeal principle. We move without thinking, and it takes great discipline to subjugate this principle. The second principal is that of the incorporeal mind, or the soul. This principle is responsible for our voluntary motions. (Letters, 243) I can sit here at my computer and type because I have consciously willed to do so. My incorporeal mind causes my fingers to push the correct keys. The incorporeal mind also makes it possible for me to sit and think, motionless, about what it is I will type. Emotions and pain are registered in the incorporeal mind, although the response may be manifest in the corporeal principle.

The situation of motion is quite different for animals, however. The incorporeal mind is completely absent in animals (although present in the human animal). This means that any motion acted out by an animal has origins in the construction of the physical organs of that animal. The squirrel foraging for acorns does so because the need for food sets off a mechanical "switch" in its body and causes it to look for food. The dogs yelps and runs away when smacked with a rolled-up newspaper because a "spring" has been set off to make it do so. Animals are not conscious of pain. In fact, it is difficult to speak of the pain of animals in the thought of Descartes simply because they do not consciously feel pain. Animals are mere machines, "automata" in Descartes' terminology, mechanically reacting to outer forces, such as the rolled-up newspaper, and inner forces, such as the physical need for food. Everything an animal does is, for Descartes, like clockwork.

Doubtless when the swallows come in spring, they operate like clocks. The actions of honeybees are of the same nature, and the discipline of cranes in flight, and of apes in fighting (Letters, 207).

Descartes gives a rather bizarre defense of his theory that animals are automata (and he admits that it is only a theory, on which we will comment later). He writes, "It seems reasonable, since art copies nature, and men make various automata which move without thought [earlier, he gives the example of clockworks], that nature should produce its own automata, much more splendid than artificial [man-made] ones. These natural automata are the animals" (Letters, 244).

Since men can make machines, then it only naturally follows that "nature" is able to produce such even more "splendid" machines.

Unfortunately for the animals, the "splendid" character of these natural clocks does not merit any respect on the part of man. "Descartes himself dissected living animals in order to advance his knowledge of anatomy" (Singer 209). In the seventeenth century, vivisection involved nailing the paws of fully conscious animals onto boards and slicing into the flesh to reveal organs (Singer, 209).

Descartes recognized the logical outcome of his view of animals; that humans do not hold any responsibility to animals without souls. "My opinion is not so much cruel to animals as indulgent to men... since it absolves them from the suspicion of crime when they eat or kill animals" (Letters, 245). For Descartes, the machine-like character of animals dissolves any moral responsibility that humans may feel they have towards animals.

To those of us familiar with even the elementary principles of physiology, it seems obvious that since animals (especially mammals) have a very similar organ structure as humans, it follows that they would also feel pain in a like manner as we humans. Now, Descartes did indeed recognize the physical similarities, but he was not willing to follow that through to attributing like experience of pain. Voltaire found this mechanical view reprehensible and inconsistent. "Answer me, mechanist, has Nature arranged all the springs of feeling in this animal to the end that it may not feel?" (Singer, 210).

How does one respond to such a strange view of animals? As Descartes says, "the human mind does not reach into their [animals'] hearts" (Letters, 244). Observing an animal writhing, it may seem that the animal is feeling pain. However, there really is no way for me to enter into its mind and know for certain whether or not it is experiencing the stimulus on a conscious level. On the other hand, there is no way for me to know for certain that the animal is not experiencing pain on a conscious level.

Descartes himself recognized that his theory could not be proven either way. Because of this recognition, he left some openings in his philosophy. Descartes admits that it "may be conjectured" that since animals have organs similarly arranged as in humans, then they have thoughts. Still, he says, these thoughts would "be of a very much less perfect kind" (Letters, 208). Descartes attributes the capacity to speak (in words or signs) to the existence of a soul, the incorporeal principle. Since animals cannot speak in any way understandable to humans, they must not possess this incorporeal principle.

[T]his proves not only that brutes have less Reason than man, but that they have none at all: for we see that very little is required to enable a person to speak. [I]t is incredible that the most perfect ape or parrot of its species, should not in this be equal to the most stupid infant, or at least to one that was crack-brained, unless the soul of brutes were of a nature wholly different from ours (Discourse on Method, 62).

In this place of ambiguity and uncertainty, I think it would be best to give the animal the benefit of the doubt. Assume that animals do indeed feel conscious pain. This assumption is not a far leap to make. Animals and humans have similar physiological structures, "springs of feeling," in the words of Voltaire, and animals react to a painful stimulus in the same way that humans do (writhing, attempting to escape the source of pain, vocalizations of protest).

Karl Rahner's writings describe a transcendent love story between a mysterious God and the special beings he created for himself. To read this Catholic theologian is to be touched by the faithfulness of his path, his wonder for his Creator, his concern for his fellow humans. To read him is also to find little room for the real value of any creature beyond these human beings.

Rahner's God is Mystery of mysteries. How many times does Rahner use that word to point toward the wonder to which he refers? God is unknowable but absolutely trustworthy. Rahner writes: Remember that God is simply the incomprehensible. That is how he is the eternal, personal, knowing, self-possessing primal cause of our existence. He is the personal God who is absolutely identical with his freedom, so that we cannot -- so to speak -- get behind this freedom of God... (231).

Yet, Rahner seemingly sees beyond the veil clearly enough to discern what constitutes God's precise concern: Us. We humans. Just as God ought to be our ultimate, our everything, so we seem to be His. Rahner describes God's activity in terms of God's monogamous fidelity to our well-being. God has created the world in order to "raise up beings who can stand in personal relationship to himself and so receive his message" (47). Only two partners -- God and humans -- are really, deeply involved in this Cosmic dance.

This exclusivity perhaps is understandable, given the human concerns with which Rahner is wrestling. He is grappling with a human anxiety, un-knowing, the fear of insignificance and of death. Rahner sees into the confusing world humans face, a human history that: seems to human beings a growing chaos -- an impenetrable mix of sin and holiness, light and darkness, of blood and tears, of noble achievements and rash presumption; a history that is appalling and magnificent, an ooze of endless trivia and yet a high drama. (195).

And it is within this same history that the human being also "is reduced to the status of total insignificance among billions of his brothers and sisters" (195). Rahner sees the woundedness of the human person, the unease with which we dwell in this world, and writes that the human is as someone dying, who is "suspended between heaven and earth, for we are not fully at home either here or there. Heaven is too remote from us, and earth too is far from being a dwelling place in which we can feel ourselves really secure" (298). Rahner is sensitive to our painful ennui, to times in which "our soul seems to continue its weary way on the road followed endlessly by the multitude with its innumerable trifles" (511). For Rahner, God answers these aches -- the lack of certainty, the fear we don't really matter, the loss of meaning. But in doing so, in assuring humans they are, indeed, beloved in a vast universe no matter how seemingly small, Rahner defines them over and against all other beings.

Rahner preaches the Good News: the word that God loves us. Through his writing, he cares for his fellow humans, promising: that the dreary plain of our existence also has peaks soaring up into the eternal light of the infinite God, peaks we can all scale, and that the awful bottomless abysses still hide God-filled depths we have not sounded, even when we think we have experienced everything and found it all absurd (389).

His care is commendable. But it casts a shadow. In order to assure his human brothers and sisters of their inestimable worth, no matter how large or confusing the world, he distinguishes them from the next-closet beings: the animals.

This is a recurring theme in Rahner's writing. Humans must not imagine they are simply part and parcel of the natural world, lest they become "an animal with technical sophistication" (82). He notes that if we ceased contemplating God we may "die a collective death and regress back into a colony of unusually resourceful animals" (208). Our human knowledge of God gives us meaning, and "without it everything is limited, every individual truth within the picture of the world becomes the prison in which the person dies the death of an animal -- although a clever one" (215). He argues that humans cannot be reduced to a mere "rational animal" (348). Doubtless Rahner did not intend to disparage the animals. The animals weren't his concern at all. He was concerned about the problem of human existence. His impulse was pastoral. But in defining who humans are, he defines who they are not. And that point of departure is where we as humans begin mattering to God -- which bodes badly for the animals.

Rahner follows this trajectory in his understanding of creation. By making humans God's most significant concern, all of creation falls into relief. This is not to say Rahner's understanding of creation was simple. In fact, it was subtle. He tried to correct a stark platonic dualism between matter and spirit, world and God, (261), and partly reconciled humans to creation. He urges humans to "love everything loved by him with his love .... precisely as something valid in the sight of God, as something eternally justified and hence as something divinely and religiously significant before God" (262). Yet Rahner quotes St. Ignatius in setting forth the world hierarchy: "The human person is created to praise, reverence, and serve God our Lord, and by that means to attain salvation. The other things on the face of the earth are created to help the person attain the end for which he is created" (89). According to this definition, not one non-human being has inherent value. Every plant, insect and animal matters only in relation to what humans want from them. Rahner, in shaping an understanding of human relationship with creation, reminds us that humans cannot succumb to nature, must not "abandon their role as the measure of all things" (82).

For all its beauty, Rahner's theology affirms an anthropocentric view of the world that offers little to nonhumans. A hawk gliding over a steep, green valley, a lioness giving birth to her young, Emily leaping a fence and fleeing into the woods -- the only relevance of these events is as they appear to us, as they might inspire or delight or frustrate us. They are nothing unto themselves.

Tillich

For animal advocates and theologians, it is regrettable, given the power and majesty of Paul Tillich's Systematic Theology, that Tillich continued the mainline Christian tradition in failing to specifically develop an animal, or 'subhuman' (in Tillich's terminology), theology. Tillich's theology is anthropocentric and perpetuates a categorical distinction between the human and the animal in delimiting the dimension of 'spirit' to the human. The hopeful animal theologian is then relegated to asking whether Tillich's system could be viewed as supportive, or at least not structurally opposed, to theological positions such as those of Schweitzer and Linzey.

In surveying the Systematic Theology to conjecture what Tillich might have written concerning the theological underpinnings of animal welfare, we may at first be disheartened by his statement that "In maintaining that the fulfillment of creation is the actualization of finite freedom, we affirm implicitly that man is the telos." (Vol 1, 258)

Man uniquely transcends the "chain of stimulus and response by deliberation and decision". Further, says Tillich, "Man is the image of God because in him the ontological elements are complete and unified on a creaturely basis, just as they are complete and united in God as the creator. Man's logos is analogous to the divine logos." (259).[xii]

Clearly Tillich draws a categorical distinction between the human and the subhuman, but one must ask whether Tillich would intend that distinction to support the Thomist conclusion of the absence of "fellowship" between the categories and the resultant absolute dominion of the human over the subhuman. Even if this were to be Tillich's answer as well, we could plausibly conjecture that Tillich might be persuaded otherwise by more recent scientific findings that would blur such a categorical distinction between instinct and reason.

However, further study within Tillich's system suggests that Tillich would dispute the Thomist conclusion. Plausible evidence for this is found in Tillich's caution that although the ontologies are incomplete in the subhuman, this does not imply that the subhuman has less "perfection". "On the contrary, man as the essentially threatened creature cannot compare with the natural perfection of the subhuman creatures." (Vol 1, 260). Here Tillich uses the same term, 'perfection', that was used by Aquinas to support a divine ordinance of beings that proceeds from imperfection to perfection where the less perfect are subject to the use and dominion of the more perfect. But Tillich extols the natural perfection of the subhuman to the human.

In Vol 3, Tillich rejects the metaphor of "levels" within creation. Here he answers 'yes" to the express question of whether there is a gradation of value among the various dimensions of creation, but only in the sense that the criterion of value is the "power of a being to include a maximum number of potentialities in one living actuality. . . . Man is the highest being within the realm of our experience, but he is by no means the most perfect." (17).

Later in this section Tillich explains that 'perfection' means actualization of one's potentialities, which can be found to be more perfectly actualized in the subhuman. Rather, then, the criteria for the ranking of the dimensions of life are the degree of 'centeredness' and the richness of its content. Man is the highest being in being a fully-centered being which is all-embracing in terms of content.

Yet it cannot be overemphasized that in Tillich's system this difference is a matter only of degree. Both centeredness and individualization are "qualities of everything that is, whether limited or fully developed (32)". Indeed, the appearance of a new dimension of life is dependent on the constellation of conditions in a preceding or lower dimension. Thus, Tillich rejects the doctrine that God added an 'immortal soul' to the human, bearing with it the life of spirit, at some discrete moment in the evolutionary process, which he says is borne out of a "supranaturalistic doctrine of man". With this rejection comes the correlative rejection of theologies debasing animal welfare on the grounds that animals, unlike man, have no 'soul'. Moreover, such a concept, asserts Tillich, disrupts the multidimensional unity of life.

The oneness of being is irrefutably foundational in Tillich's system. Even if one is not persuaded of a qualitative distinction with a moral difference between the Thomist ordering of nature and Tillich's multidimensionality, then the animal theologian can turn with hope to the interdependent unity of being in Tillich's system. God's directing creativity creates through the freedom of man and through the "spontaneity and structural wholeness of all creatures" (Vol. 1, 266) and man actualizes his finite freedom in unity with the whole of reality. Tillich expressly rejects the classical doctrine that man participates in nature as a microcosmos: "What happens in the microcosm happens by mutual participation in the macrocosmos, for being itself is one" (261). While this interdependence may not give the moral mileage to get us to Schweitzer's concept of reverence for life, it certainly implies that man may interfere with the telos of the subhuman at his peril.

Tillich believes that the question of man's participation in the subhuman becomes most crucial in the consideration of whether the Christian doctrine of salvation of the 'world' refers to the human race alone. Clearly, Tillich agrees with classical doctrine that salvation is cosmic and universal because "the totality of being demands a participation of the universe in salvation" (Vol. 2, 96). While it is the eternal relation of God to man that is made manifest in the Christ, "man cannot claim that the infinite has entered the finite to overcome its existential estrangement in mankind alone" (96), although such is beyond verification by man. Tillich suggests that where there may be an awareness of existential estrangement in non-human worlds, the interdependence of the totality of being requires the operation of saving power within such worlds. Linzey mistakenly grasps this point to claim that Tillich includes animals within the reconciling work of Christ.[xiii] Yet, although Tillich does not go this far, his system demands that the subhuman participates in God's salvation.

Although the lodestar of Tillich's system is humanity and its essential estrangement, it cannot reasonably be viewed as supportive of the Thomist doctrine regarding animals. While the human remains the 'highest being', this ascendant position derives from an evolved degree of actualization of the potential dimensions of life, not in a momentary divine bestowal of innate superiority, and humanity remains embedded within the interdependent multidimensional unity of life. Clearly Tillich would support ecologically based protection of the subhuman world as necessary for humanity and consonant with God's salvation.

A Theological Analysis: Seeking an Animal Inclusive Theology

"Not to hurt our humble brethren (the animals) is our first duty to them, but to stop there is not enough. We have a higher mission – to be of service to them whenever they require it. If you have men who will exclude any of God's creatures from the shelter of compassion and pity, you will have men who will deal likewise with their fellow men." St. Francis of Assisi

While a vast majority of Christian theology has been indifferent to animal issues (such as Tillich) or outrightly harmful to the animal rights cause (such as Descartes), other theologians have recognized this particular deficit and sought to do something about it. Even in works by more helpful theologians, systems do not always include an explicit theology of animals. Therefore, we must at times construct an animal theology in addition to conducting an analysis. Such is the case with, for example, Marjorie Suchocki.

Analyzing Emily's Story via Marjorie Suchocki and Carol Adams

Conventional theology may see Emily's leap to freedom and the subsequent human hoopla a diversion largely devoid of godly significance. By intertwining the process theology of Marjorie Suchocki and Carol Adams' feminist critique of theology, however, we can tell a story rich with theological meaning. In this story, Emily's life does indeed matter in the world and to God. And her story reveals the possibility of healing the broken relationship between humans and the rest of creation.

Uncovering the Power Bias Suchocki's and Adams' feminist perspective helps them illumine traditional theology's blindness: location and power influence theological conclusions. Suchocki points out that privileged and powerful humans develop systems of thinking that reinforce their power, to the detriment of groups such as women and African Americans (3). Adams in Neither Man Nor Beast brings this point to bear on Emily's story. Emily had been excluded from human care because humans have decided that she does not "matter" in the same way humans do. She was sent to the slaughterhouse on the assumption that her body belongs to humans, and we may do to her what we wish. Theology has aided that conclusion by arguing from special abilities such as language -- which supposedly place humans nearer to God. Adams points out that this is "circular" thinking -- humans beginning with human capacities to define what is special to God. Adams says: "Language may be one of the methods for acquiring knowledge, but to stake one's knowledge claims solely on language becomes self-referential ... anthropocentric theology is inherently circular too" (182). Humans have made "absolute knowledge claims" regarding categories of beings, including animals. "Such Absolute or universal knowledge claims," Adams writes, "represent the logic and interest of the oppressor" (188). Adams recounts how she came to "know" in her body that we shouldn't torture and kill animals, which "involved recognizing that whereas I had ontologized animals as consumable, exploitable, violable, I could do so only through the god trick, by following the methods of any oppressor in believing the illusions that this was a universal perspective" (193).

Adams additionally suggests that anthropocentric God metaphors often assert a "triumphant, monarchical God" that "help to explain why we see animals as exploitable. A value hierarchy that is upheld by a logic of domination places animals so low on the hierarchy that their bodies can be viewed instrumentally" (185). Process theology abandons traditional ideas of omnipotence, which helps us to envision different, more companionable metaphors - metaphors that could enable us to include animals within that which we hold sacred.

Everything Matters in Process: Bringing Emily into God's Being

Suchocki envisions for us a reality which includes everything in it, and in which everything effects God. According to Suchocki, the world works this way: God envisions in God's primordial nature an infinite number of possibilities held together by a vision of harmony (30-31). The world is made up from occasions of experience which God summons toward the most harmonious choice. When those occasions are completed, they become what is actual, and God accepts these into God's being. Suchocki's world is eminently relational - everything has an impact, which God feels. Once a "unit of existence" is complete, it becomes an influence in the ongoing process (30-36). Suchocki does not limit this influence to humans. She writes that "in a relational world, no entity, be it cell or society, can exist apart from its receiving and giving to others" (76). No one and no event stands in isolation: not the song of the cricket, the event of a child's new tooth, a colt's first, wobbly steps. So the well-being of all beings matter. "To be for oneself," Suchocki writes, "is also to be for others" (82).

God feels all of the world's happenings - not just that which impacts humans. "God feels this world, not as an abstraction, but as a reality" (109). Everything that has become will register in what we might call the body of God (81). There is a horror in this. To understand this means to know that at this moment God feels whatever the billions of animals experience as they are crowded into cages, or tossed into trashbags, or herded into slaughterhouse-bound trucks. God feels, then, the pigs freezing in the truck on their way to slaughter, as described by a worker in Gail Eisnitz' book.

They're supposed to be dead when they come back there. I thought, anyway. I went to pick up some hogs one day for chain sawing from a pile of about thirty frozen hogs, and I found two frozen hogs alive in that pile.... I could tell they were alive because they raised their heads up like, 'Help me.' Like they were saying 'Somebody's got to have to do something to help me.' (103).

Suchocki writes that "the dreadful truth revealed in crucifixion of Jesus Christ is that the world crucified God. We crucify God. Each pain we feel and each pain we inflict enters into the reality of the God who is for us" (110). There are moments of joy, though, and relief, as in the moment of Emily's escape. God was with Emily -- felt Emily -- as she faced her slaughter. And God was with her as she leaped over the five-foot high fence and sought some measure of freedom. God feels Emily now, as she lives contented and in peace.

Slaughtering Animals as Sin; Breaking the Grip of Sin

If Adams is right, and animals are to be accorded a status previously denied in anthropocentric theology, then we see our system of treating animals in a new, harsh light. If animals are subjects, we wrongly treat them as objects -- and introduce sin into the world. Suchocki writes the societal sin occurs when "any society treats others, within or without, as objects for its own disposal" (121). Suchocki notes that we are born into the structures of the world as they are. Americans are born into a world in which burgers on the grill are the norm. Slaughterhouse workers are born into towns where killing animals one of the few available jobs. Factory farm owners are born into a world that considers animals objects to be used for our convenience. This is all the state of sin. Suchocki writes: We are born into structures that already shape our existence, molding our identity. We absorb these structures into our normal way of perceiving things, so that we are not only shaped by the structures, but we perpetuate them (193).

One step toward healing this state of societal sin, according to Suchocki, is to name the "demons" (194) -- to see how we all contribute toward sinful structure. For us, this means naming Speciesism -- the sinful state that lets us see Emily -- a living, breathing, sentient being -- as a tool for our use, an object to please our palates.

God always urges us to include more of the world in our understanding of our essential relationality. "We are pushed not so much toward an awareness of God as we are toward a deeper awareness of the world and its interrelationships ... the reign of God looks toward a gracious inclusiveness towards all people and all nations, and toward an abundance in the natural world," Suchocki writes (191). Emily's escape works to that end. The event brought attention to a particular cow, and a cow's life. People flock to the Peace Abbey with their children to meet Emily, and to listen to her story. While they are at the Abbey they learn about a peaceful, vegetarian diet that embraces all living beings. Animals become more "real" for people visiting the Abbey. Emily helps accomplish an increased awareness of the relationality of beings, to use Suchocki's concepts.

Emily similarly helps create what Adams calls a "Second-Person Theology" - that is, a theology constructed out of an actual relationship with those beings whom we are describing in our theology. Adams writes: God unfolds in relationships. Most animals are excluded from experiencing this notion of "God-in-relationship" because we use them in ways that sever relationships. Many forms of animal exploitation involve caging and confining them, restricting their ability -- no, their need -- to enjoy social relationships, and bestow upon animals an expectation that they can exist inanimately even while alive .... If God is in process, being, and revealed through relationship should we not situate all beings within the divine relationship, seeing with loving eyes? (195).

In this theology, we would experience animals outside of situations in which they are exploited -- farming, circuses, laboratories, hunting expeditions -- so that we could actually understand who they are in relation to us, and perhaps get a better sense of who they might be to God. This is the kind of knowing that people such as Jane Goodall has experienced. As Adams questions, how do we say who animals are, or aren't, when we don't really know them? Emily is providing such an opportunity now.

Seeing Past the Blindness

Though Suchocki presents a way of understanding Emily's situation theologically, Suchocki is not a perfectly animal-friendly theologian. She, too, often speaks in terms of human society when referring to justice. She refers to two general categories: humans, and a vague, general nature, writing, for example that "we realize that we, too, are nature, and that our caring cannot be restricted to sisters and brothers in the human community, but must extend toward 'brother sun and sister moon,' and all the earth and sky" (195). Like many ecologically minded humans, she jumps from considering the worth of individual humans to a very general "nature", and skips commenting upon individual animals within nature.[xiv] Likewise, she focuses upon human "consciousness" as God's highest value (46). In short, while she constructs a theology in which she sees how we humans fail to notice our blindness, she herself does not fully see. Yet, she also provides the possibility of an eventual realization.

Suchocki says to achieve God's reign on earth, we must be listen for new and unexpected forms of God's call for justice. She speaks squarely to a religious sensibility that defends slaughtering animals because the Bible says we can, or because old theologians said we ought. She writes: Our natural tendency is to draw back from new ways of actualizing justice, for we would rather hold on to the security of the past. But the reign of God does not allow us that luxury. Our trust must not be placed in our past ways, not even when those ways were enacted in response to concrete divine guidance. This would be akin to a person at age forty claiming that seven-year-old behavior was still appropriate, since once it had been in response to God's guidance. (192).

How much of our mistreatment of animals like Emily flows merely from past assumptions? From the status quo?

By escaping, Emily startled the status quo. She gave human beings an opportunity to consider as an individual a being typically treated as a thing. In doing so, she created a chance for healing in our relationships with the animals, and the rest of the nonhuman world.

Schweitzer

Schweitzer felt that theology and philosophy of the past had overlooked animal issues, resulting in grave consequences. On Descartes, Schweitzer writes that he has "bewitched all of modern philosophy;" "We might say that philosophy has played a piano of which a whole series of keys were considered untouchable" (Teaching, 50). This series of keys is, of course, the issue of non-human animals. Schweitzer wants to start playing these keys.

Schweitzer takes quite a different approach to his analysis of animals. In fact, one could say that he doesn't "analyze" animals. He doesn't engage in the deconstruction of the psyche into different principals. Schweitzer's concern is with life, not corporeal or incorporeal principles.

For Schweitzer, life in and of itself is worthy of respect. He calls this idea "the ethics of reverence for life."

Reverence for life in an all-encompassing ethic. It includes humans, "lower" animals, and even plant life. Reverence for life expresses itself in compassion for all life. Under reverence for life, "the essence of Goodness is: Preserve life, promote life, help life to achieve its highest destiny. The essence of Evil is: Destroy life, harm life, hamper the development of life" (Teaching, 26). In rescuing Emily the cow from the slaughterhouse, and in their vegan lifestyle, the Randas were in line with reverence for life. They sought to preserve Emily rather than destroy her, to promote her rather than harm her, to allow her to live out her natural life free from the threat of slaughter.

For Schweitzer, we have responsibility to treat all life with equal respect. "The ethics of reverence for life makes no distinction between higher and lower, more precious and less precious lives" (Teaching, 47). All life is considered to be of equal value under the ethics of reverence for life. This raises some problems. If we are not to distinguish between higher and lower forms of life, what are we to do when there are irreconcilable conflicts of interests? What am I to do with mice or ants in my kitchen? I have an interest in keeping a sanitary space in which to eat and live, and this cannot be maintained while mice eat my bread and ants crawl in my sugar bowl.

Schweitzer does not try to gloss over the fact that it is necessary to destroy some form of life to protect or promote the interests of another form of life. There is no way to get around this fact. The answer lies in dealing with this unpleasantry with integrity. "When under pressure of necessity, the truly ethical man is forced to decide which life will be sacrificed in order to preserve other lives, he realizes that he is proceeding subjectively and ultimately arbitrarily, and that he is accountable for the lives sacrificed (Teaching, 47)." When possible, we should do all we can to avoid harming life. When this ideal is not possible, we must be willing to take responsibility for our actions.

For Schweitzer, peace between humans and animals is essential to peace between humans: "A system of values which concerns itself only with our relationship to other people is incomplete and therefore lacking in power and good. Only by means of reverence for life can we establish a spiritual and humane relationship with both people and all living creatures within our reach" (Reverence, 57).

When humans exclude animals from ethical treatment, human ethical development is stunted. "Through reverence for life, we become, in effect, different persons" (Reverence, 57). By affirming the inherent value of life, one enters into a new relationship with the universe, allowing one to "act on a higher plane, because we feel ourselves truly at home in our world" (Reverence, 57). Schweitzer's reverence for life extends beyond a sense of allegiance to the human species, and therefore allows one to care for the human species at a deeper level. For Schweitzer, reverence for life had political implications. On atomic weapons, he writes, "The abolition of atomic weapons will become possible only if world opinion demands it. And the spirit needed to achieve this end can be created only by reverence for life" (Reverence, 62). Schweitzer offers us a new way to look at the world. Through reverence for life, we are freed to have truly peaceful relations with all of God's creation.

Linzey One may well question whether theology or any theological perspective was influential in motivating the sympathetic, or perhaps empathetic, responses to Emily. The theologian Andrew Linzey has authored several works in his effort to develop a Christian theology of animal rights. In his Christianity and the Rights of Animals[xv], Linzey concludes that despite a strongly influential Thomistic tradition of justifying man's absolute dominion over non-human creation based upon a naturalistic order of creation, Christianity is not "irremediably specieist".[xvi] Rather, Christianity has not squarely addressed the question of the theological significance of animals; systematic theology regarding animals has yet to be done. It cannot surprise us, then, if theology has figured insignificantly in secular thinking about animals and their plight.

In his effort to add theological argument to humanistic, psychological, ecological and other grounds for animal welfare, Linzey has charted much of the territory centered on a God-perspective approach. Though compact and concise, Christianity and the Rights of Animals touches on most of the elements of a systematic assay, the ethos of which is expressed in an exhortative proposition borrowed from Romans: "The groaning and travailing of creation awaits the inspired sons of God"[xvii].

Clearly this proposition implies that humanity should play a significant role in the redemption of non-human creation, but Linzey's perspective is not simply humanist. The "theos-rights' of animals, as conceived by Linzey, are not given by humanity but by God. To affirm that animals possess rights means (1) that God as creator has rights in his creation; (2) that "Spirit-filled breathing creatures composed of flesh and blood"[xviii] are subjects of inherent value to God; and, (3) the foregoing assertions are the ground of an objective moral claim which is nothing less than God's claim on us. Against the charge that 'rights' conceptions are intrinsically untheological, Linzey argues that even the concept of human rights must ultimately be grounded theistically; non-human creatures (at least those Spirit-filled breathing creatures composed of flesh and blood, which category would include Emily) then have the same claim as humanity to be honored and respected as that which God has given.

At the foundation of Linzey's animal theology, then, is the ontological fact of creation, the "giveness of created reality"[xix] and the critically important theological assertion that God cares, despite the equally apparent ontological fact that nature, even without human tyranny, is red in tooth and claw. Linzey's God-perspective is fundamentally grounded in his hermeneutics of the Genesis story and of the new covenant made by God through Jesus Christ. Creation, and the place of the human and non-human within it, is to be understood within the duality of blessing and curse. The blessedness of creation is understood in God's generosity in creating, in the independent intrinsic value of all creation as it partakes of the divine glory (necessitating bovine glory), and the God-given freedom of each of God's creatures to enjoy their life with and in God in relation to their nature and according to their being.

The curse of creation inheres in its fallen state: all of creation, not only humanity Linzey emphasizes, is estranged from God. The cursedness of this state of alienation is manifest particularly in the 'risk of creation', the freedom of creatures, especially the human, to turn against creation and in the "shackles of mortality" binding all creatures.[xx]

Yet, as Christians, we know that God has wrought reconciliation and redemption in Jesus Christ. But Linzey reminds us, in contrast with anthropocentric (and soteriologically anthropomonistic) Christian theological tradition, that just as all creation fell, all creation is redeemed. Humanity then, is to be concerned not only with its own salvation but also with the salvation of all creation. The basis and nature of that concern is articulated by the biblical concepts of 'dominion' and 'covenant'.

The Thomistic view of absolute dominion (radah in Hebrew) over non-human creation conflicts threefold with a scholarly analysis of the Genesis story (Genesis 1:26 et seq): first, man's lordship is dependent upon and derivative of the absolute power of God and his dominion is therefore to be God-like; second' man's 'kingship' is exercised in accountability to God and the kingdom is to be founded on God's order (differing presumably from the Thomistic conception); and, third, man's bodily sustenance is to be the plants and fruit-bearing trees[xxi], further evidence of God's will that man's dominance not be absolute (and will not extend to devouring Emily).

If dominion is dependent, how should such dominion be exercised? Linzey asserts that our model must be God's self-revealed life in Jesus Christ expressed in humility, service and sacrificial love. Indeed, although Linzey admits that little can be gleaned from the gospels to construct Jesus' view toward animals, he posits that Jesus' special concern for the 'least among us' impresses humanity with a special trust for non-human creation.

Human responsibility toward non-human creation and animals particularly is also explicitly derived from God's covenant. In Genesis 9:8-11, God makes his covenant with man and with "every living creature that is with you." Humanity is thus placed in a moral community with other living creatures and is bound to a moral covenant with animals. Further, argues Linzey, centuries of Christian theology have institutionalized an anthropomorphic redemption when a cosmic redemption was foreordained in the Old Testament. The Incarnation is not God's "special 'yes' to human beings"[xxii]. Linzey counters that the 'ousia' assumed in the Incarnation is of all creaturely being. Although man's rational and self-conscious nature comports with a biblical view that man may achieve a greater intimacy with God, rationality is not the sine qua non for spiritual status. The same breath of Spirit (ruach) breathes life into man and animal alike – our redemption is also theirs.

How, then, should humanity cooperate with God the Spirit in the redemption of creation, in the "freeing of creation to be itself for God"[xxiii]? Linzey offers three opportunities: the adoption of an attitude of reverence for the grace of created life; the substitution of God-centeredness for anthropocentricity in valuing creation; and the surrender of human hubris and meddling. If we can do no good, then at least do no harm; we should let creation be as God intended.

With respect to Spirit-filled creatures composed of flesh and blood, like Emily, Linzey's behavioral translation of the above moral precepts is the "liberation" of these creatures from "wanton injury". Wanton actions are those devoid of moral justification like 'need', 'defense', 'survival' or even 'benefit'. 'Injury' inheres in any activity that causes pain, suffering, harm, distress, deprivation or death.

With this moral armor, donned in defense of his theologically grounded animal theos-rights[xxiv], Linzey assails humanity's treatment of animals in specific instances, including the predicament of Emily and her kin. To the extreme confinement practices of intensive farming and the suffering engendered thereby, we must respond that all Emilys have the God-given right to be cows, to live their God-intended natural life without perversion simply for human gain. Whether or not some would argue that humans have a 'need' for meat (an argument that Linzey and we would consider unsupportable), there is no right to the cheapest meat or the whitest veal that trumps the animal's right to its natural life (its telos).

With respect to the morality of eating meat, Linzey recognizes that Genesis 9.3 ('Every creature that lives and moves shall be food for you; I give you them all as I once gave you all green plants') apparently revokes the vegetarian limitation in God's gift of food in Genesis 1:29. Linzey argues that notion that the animal's life belongs only to God is retained in the stricture of Genesis 9:4: 'But you must not eat the flesh with the life, which is the blood, still in it'. Although the priestly tradition accepted meat eating that may have been, Linzey conjectures, necessary to survival at the time, the tradition did not sanction human appropriation of the life of the animal. The moral significance of taking the life of the animal is preserved and can only be justified when essential to human survival. Our mistake in interpreting Genesis 9:3-4 has been to allow an exception to establish a permanent rule. If the biblical notion that the life of an animal belongs to God is accepted and it is also recognized that humans do not need to kill for food in order to sustain health or even to eat well, then the slaughterhouse cannot possibly be morally condoned. "For if luxury rather than necessity can justify killing, where will it all end?"[xxv]

Conclusion

We began this effort with several assumptions: theology has the power to influence human thinking about our relationships with others; the animals are in dire need of theological consideration; and traditional theology fails to come to their aid. We sought a theology that includes them in our care.

Each of the final group of theologians we explored provided rich resources with which to reconsider the animals, and therefore conduct a proper theological analysis of Emily and her escape. Schweitzer is lyrical and deeply empathic. His strength flows from his inclusiveness, the beauty of his language, his earnest concern. Schweitzer rightly points out the need for humans to consider the animals if they wish to have real peace on earth -- and so speaks strongly to the wisdom of the impulse to cheer Emily on, as so many in her neighborhood did when she escaped.

Linzey's Biblical reconsideration of the animals is potent when we consider how much abuse of the animals is Biblically based. He provides an understanding of how Emily by escaping was fulfilling her God-given telos and establishes her theos-right to do so. Marjorie Suchocki provides a vibrant theology that speaks to a new consciousness about relationality, and enables us to see how each being is affected by other beings. Her language, as well as Linzey's formulation of theos-rights, enables us to frame the abuse of animals in terms of sin, and Emily's rescue as part of a new consciousness -- a new word from God about justice.

Our ideal theology based on these theologians, however, would be a blend of Suchocki and Linzey. We would join Suchocki's dynamic relationality with Linzey's recognition of God's love for and rights in the animals of His creation. The result would be a theology of relationality elevated to include the theos-rights of animals -- a theology that does not reduce relationality only to animal welfare, but that also recognizes each animal's telos and its God-given right to actualize that telos. We would call for a theology that recognizes that we are all connected -- we who walk or crawl or fly, humans and dolphins and Emily -- and each within that web ought to live out its God-intended life.

CPSIA information can be obtained at www.ICGtesting.com
Printed in the USA
BVOW061433110512

290006BV00001B/99/A